KNOWING KNOWLEDGE

ONE WEEK LOAN

TABLE OF CONTENTS

THANK YOU...

Many individuals contributed (or sacrificed) time to this project.
In particular, I would like to say thanks to family (my wife Karen and children Alysha, Jared, and Kariel) for tolerating holidays whining about lack of internet access, evenings of distracted conversations, and the numerous obtuse ideas dropped upon unsuspecting recipients.

My thinking has been very public for over five years (www.elearnspace.org). Thank you to those who have read and provided feedback on countless articles and blog postings. Your time reading and commenting has been an encouragement and important learning process for me.

Stepping out into alternative means of expressing thoughts (through online publishing, instead of traditional journals), is an act of optimism that has been modeled and directed with other transparent thinkers. One needs to abandon notions of perfection to attempt online dialogue—warts, poor sentence structure, quickly jotted thoughts, embarrassingly simple viewpoints—are kept and preserved by search engines and archives. Those who hold to product views of learning and knowledge, instead of process views, find the unforgiving nature of archives intimidating. I thank my fellow sojourners for their effort in walking new paths: Stephen Downes, Jay Cross, Will Richardson, and Maish Nichani.

Special thanks as well to those who have taken the time to provide reviews of the thoughts contained in text. Those who previously held the power to filter content are finding a diminishing world as many are now able to create, validate, and share freely. The review efforts, thoughts, guidance, advice, and input of these people are invaluable: Zaid Ali Alsagoff, Wayne Batchelder, Doug Belshaw, Mark Berthelemy, Alison Bickford, Stephen Downes, Patricia Duebel, Denham Grey, Bill Hall, David Hawkes, Pam Hook, David Lee, Karla Lopez, Corrado Petrucco, John D. Smith, Susan Spero, Louise Starkey, Liz Stevenson, Peter Tittenberger, John Veitch, Jack Vinson, Peter West, Gerry White, Terry Yelmene, Steve Yurkiw, and Christopher Zielinski.

Thanks to Euan Semple, Dave Snowden, and Denham Grey for interview/online discussions relating to knowledge in our world today.

The images in this book are the work of Murray Toews. I spent much time with him in creating a non-structured, non-linear model for expressing key concepts. I have read too many books on knowledge and knowledge management that assume advanced theories must be expressed in complex, intimidating images. Structure does not equate with knowledge (structure is quite different from organization).

As an active participant in the transparent world of online writing, I know the value of building on the work of others. I have tried to cite original ideas (I went through the painful process of trying to locate origins of popular quotes—a task not readily achieved, beyond linking to a quote database). The rapidly evolving nature of knowledge sometimes results in areas being overlooked. If you find expressions in this text that have not been sourced, please let me know.

The onerous task of editing fell on Karen Graham...

Thank You

The First Step toward Knowledge is to Know that We are Ignorant.

Richard Cecil [1]

PREFACE

Knowledge has changed; from categorization and hierarchies, to networks and ecologies. This changes everything and emphasizes the need to change the spaces and structures of our organizations.

- How do we run a meeting?
  - How do we decide on action items?
    - How do we create our marketing plan?
    - How do we learn? How do we share knowledge?
    - How do we define organizational ethics?
  - How do we foster democracy?
- How do we achieve our strategic goals?

We supposedly exist in a knowledge era. Our work and our lives center on the creation, communication, and application of knowledge.

- But what IS knowledge?
  - How is it CREATED?
  - How is it SHARED?

How does knowledge flow through our organizations today? Is it different than it was

- 10 years ago?
- 50 years ago?
- A century ago?

What does our Future hold as a Knowledge-Based Society?

Why does so much of our society look as it did in the past? Our schools, our government, our religious organizations, our media—while more complex, have maintained their general structure and shape. Classroom structure today, with the exception of a computer or an LCD projector, looks remarkably unchanged—teacher at the front, students in rows. Our business processes are still built on theories and viewpoints that existed over a century ago (with periodic amendments from thinkers like Drucker[2]). In essence, we have transferred (not transformed) our physical identity to online spaces and structures.

This book seeks to tackle knowledge—not to provide a definition—but to provide a way of seeing trends developing in the world today. Due to the changed context and characteristics of knowledge, traditional definitions are no longer adequate. Language produces different meaning for different people. The meaning generated by a single definition is not sufficiently reflective of knowledge as a whole.

We are able to *describe,* not *define* knowledge.[3]

Most leaders today would settle for a view of knowledge that enables them to take action consistent with core changes—so their organizations do not suffer from outdated actions.

Knowledge possesses two broad characteristics:

1. It describes or explains some part of the world (how atoms act, which companies to invest in for future growth, how diseases are spread),

2. We can use it in some type of action (building particle accelerators, investing, preventing disease).

All Knowledge is Information,

but NOT all Information is Knowledge.

It is my hope that this book will not be seen as a product, but rather an invitation to dialogue and debate. You can discuss the book at the **www.knowingknowledge.com** website. Articles, interviews, and news on the changing context and characteristics of knowledge will be available as well. Readers are invited to share their comments on the book or assist in re-writing it in the wiki.

I have intentionally left thoughts unstructured and unconnected, allowing readers to create their own connections.

It is not intended to be read as a comprehensive treatise on society's changes. It is designed to mimic the chaotic, complex, but holistic, nature of knowledge (and learning) in today's organizations— an attempt to duplicate knowledge in form, not only content.

I have mirrored the nature of knowledge today through text.

I have resisted the urge to extensively classify concepts.

Today, individuals stitch and weave their own networks.

The practice of **CLASSIFICATION,** as means to reduce cognitive load, ends up more taxing when it fails to accurately reflect the **UNDERLYING CORE.**

Writing in a linear format is challenging!

I am used to writing in hypertext.
Concepts relate to other concepts—but not in a linear manner.
For example, when addressing connectivism as a changed theory of learning, I want to relate it to implementation, or when addressing changes in the context in which knowledge occurs, I want to connect to changes in knowledge characteristics—but without continual repetition. Books do not work that way. To achieve the same effect in a book, I would have to rewrite (and you would have to reread) my thoughts numerous times in numerous places. The repetition would be annoying. I introduce similar concepts in various places to show connections.

Viewing learning and knowledge as network phenomena alters much of how we have experienced knowledge in the last century. Networks are adaptive, fluid, and readily scale in size and scope. A *hierarchy imposes* structure, while *networks reflect* structure.

Mass media and education, for example, have been largely designed on a one-way flow model (structure imposed by hierarchy). Hierarchies, unlike networks and ecologies, do not permit rapid adaptation to trends outside of established structure. Structure is created by a select few and imposed on the many.

The newspaper publishes, we consume.

The teacher instructs, we learn.

The news is broadcast, we listen.

An alternative to this one-way model has been developing momentum over the last few years. Simple, social, end-user control tools (blogs,[4] wikis,[5] tagging and social bookmarking,[6] podcasting,[7] video logging[8]) are affording new methods of information connection and back-flow to the original source. Feedback is more common in media and advertising than in education...but academics are beginning to see increased desire from learners to engage, not only consume, learning materials and concepts.

AS GOES **KNOWLEDGE,**
SO GO OUR **ORGANIZATIONS**

This book intends to serve 5 broad purposes:

ONE   To conceptualize learning and knowing as connection-based processes;

TWO   To explore the nature of change in the context in which knowledge exists;

THREE   To explore the change in the characteristics of knowledge itself;

FOUR   To present knowledge as a context-game—a dance that requires multiple realities, each selected to serve the intended needs of each task, challenge, or opportunity;

FIVE   To present a model for the spaces and structures which will serve the needs of our organizations (schools, universities, and corporations) for tomorrow.

KNOWING KNOWLEDGE is divided into **2** distinct sections.

SECTION ONE provides a chaotic exploration of knowledge and associated concerns. The exploration of learning, connectivism, and connective knowledge forms a lens through which we can see and understand trends impacting learning and knowledge development. The *theoretical basis of learning* is presented in this section.

SECTION TWO provides a description of the changes relating to knowledge today. Implications of changes, suggested revisions to spaces and structures of our society and corporations, and models for implementing are suggested. The *practical basis of connectivism* is presented in this section.

Knowing Knowledge is directed at two broad audiences:

Educators   &   *Business Leaders*
(designers, instructors,
and administration)

While this may be an interesting pairing of target audience, it extends from my assertion that life is a learning/knowledge-based process. Literacy, marketing, leading, producing, instructing—in our developing knowledge society, these tasks require knowledge. Anyone who works with knowledge needs to be acquainted with learning processes.

A business executive needs to understand the characteristics of knowledge that impact creating effective teams to achieve corporate strategy. An educator needs to understand the new context of knowledge in order to prepare learners for a life of learning and working with knowledge. Simply put, life is learning. If we are interacting with people, ideas, or concepts (in a classroom or corporate boardroom), knowing and learning are our constant companions.

> *Whoever undertakes*
> *to set himself up*
> *as a judge of*
> *Truth and Knowledge*
> *is shipwrecked by*
> *the laughter of the gods.*
>
> Albert Einstein[9]

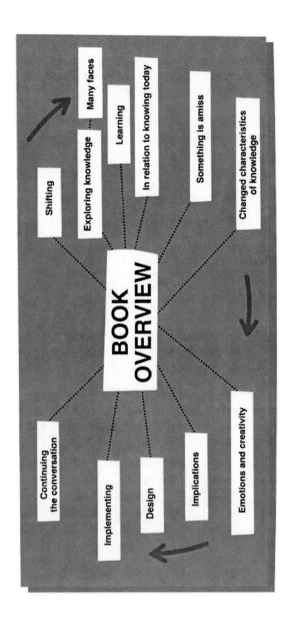

Figure 1: Book Overview[10]

An exploration

OF
THEORETICAL
views
of KNOWING
and LEARNING

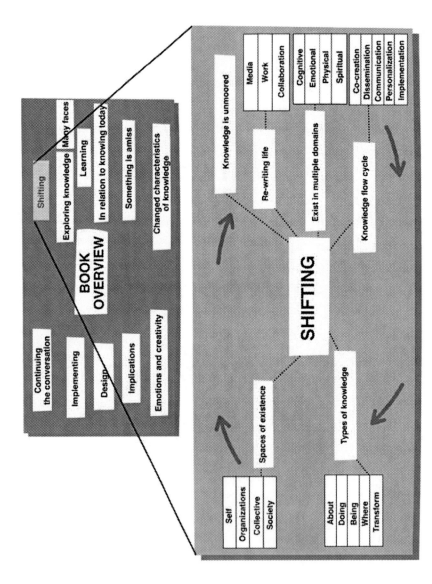

Figure 2. Introduction

SHIFTING . . .

Changes do not manifest themselves significantly in society until they are of sufficient weight and force. The building of many small, individual changes requires long periods of time before fundamental change occurs.[11] Our conceptual world view of knowledge—static, organized, and defined by experts—is in the process of being replaced by a more dynamic and multi-faceted view.

Knowledge has broken free from its moorings, its shackles. Those, like Francis Bacon, who equate knowledge with power, find that the masses are flooding the pools and reservoirs of the elite. The filters, gatekeepers, and organizers are awakening to a sea of change that leaves them adrift, clinging to their old methods of creating, controlling, and distributing knowledge.

We are in the early stages of dramatic change—change that will shake the spaces and structures of our society. Knowledge, the building block of tomorrow, is riding a tumultuous sea of change. Previously, knowledge served the aims of the economy—creation, production, and marketing. Today, knowledge is the economy. What used to be the means has today become the end.

Left in the wake of cataclysmic change are the knowledge creation and holding structures of the past. The ideologies and philosophies of reality and knowing—battle spaces of thought and theory for the last several millennia—have fallen as guides. Libraries, schools, businesses—engines of productivity and society—are stretching under the heavy burden of change. New epistemological and ontological theories are being formed, as we will discuss shortly with *connective knowledge*. These changes do not wash away previous definitions of knowledge, but instead serve as the fertile top of multiple soil layers.

The task of this book is to provide an overview of what is happening to knowledge and to the spaces in which knowledge is created, disseminated, shared, and utilized.

The pursuit of knowledge is ongoing. Unlike most desires, this desire is insatiable.[12] We tinker with the constructs of reality: What causes weather patterns? Why did it (pick any event) happen? What is that (pick any phenomenon)? If we change this, how does it impact that?

Human existence is a quest to understand. Our spaces and structures need to be aligned with our new understanding of knowledge…and the manner in which it moves, flows, and behaves.

We live as an integrated experience—we see, know, and function in connections. Life, like knowing, is not an isolated activity—it is a rich, interconnected part of who we are. We cannot stop the desire to know. The desire to know is balanced with our desire to communicate, to share, to connect, and our desire to make sense, to understand—to know the meaning. In an effort to make ourselves understood, we create structures to hold our knowledge: hierarchies, books, libraries, encyclopedias, the internet, search engines. We create spaces where we can dialogue about and enact knowledge: corporations, organizations, schools, universities, societies. And we create tools to disseminate knowledge: peer-review journals, discussion panels, conferences.

The last decade has fundamentally re-written how we:

+ Consume media
+ Authenticate and validate knowledge
+ Express ourselves and our ideas
+ Relate to information/knowledge (the relationship time is much shorter–compare 1/2 hour reading the morning newspaper vs. reading 50 news sources online in 10 minutes)
+ Relate to the deluge of information, requiring that we become much more selective and that we start using external resources (social bookmarking, user-generated and filtered content, personal tagging) to cope
+ Function in knowledge-intense environments (mass movement to knowledge-based work, diminishing physical or industrial work activities).

What has caused knowledge to leave the safe, trusted spaces of generations past?

Changes are occurring on several levels:

The context (or environment) in which knowledge exists; and

The flow and characteristics of knowledge itself.

What is the impact of KNOWLEDGE SET FREE?

The most substantial changes will be felt in how we organize ourselves. The spaces and structures of society—corporations, churches and religious bodies, schools, and government—will experience a different relationship with knowledge. Instead of relationships of control/monitor and cause/effect, these organizations require a shift in view to foster, nurture, and connect. Customers, students, and clients no longer tolerate pre-packaging (music, news, media). Knowledge set free enables dynamic, adaptive, and personalized experiences.

Yochai Benkler, in his exploration of the growing prominence of networks in society, offers a glimpse into what is at stake in our world of morphing knowledge:

Information, knowledge, and culture are central to human freedom and human development. How they are produced and exchanged in our society critically affects the ways we see the state of the world as it is and might be...for more than 150 years, modern complex democracies have depended in large measure on an industrial information economy for these basic functions. In the past decade and a half, we have begun to see a radical change in the organization of information production.[13]

These changes are still being interpreted through existing beliefs of how we should structure our organizations and what it means to know and learn. How deep must change penetrate our organizations before we see systemic change? The first attempt at implementation usually involves forcing decentralized processes into centralized models.

We stand with our feet in two worlds: one in the models and structures that originated in (and served well) the industrial era, and the second within the emerging processes and functions of knowledge flow in our era today. Our dual existence is noticed in business, education, and media—we have new tools being used to serve old needs. This phenomenon was found in the early days of video. Initially, video was thought to be best suited for taping and recording live stage shows. Video was seen as a second-rate experience to live shows. Over time, once producers and editors understood the uniqueness of the medium, video developed into its own art form.

Or consider email in its earlier days—many printed out a paper copy of emails, at least the important ones, and filed them in a file cabinet. Today we are beginning to see a shift with email products that archive and make email searchable and allow individuals to apply metadata at point of use (tagging).

Similarly, we are in the in-between stage of organizational models—we are trying to force the changed context and expressions of knowledge into structures and processes that served a previous age.

KNOWLEDGE IS NOT STATIC.

The knowledge flow cycle (see Figure 3) begins with some type of knowledge creation (individual, group, organization) and then moves through the following stages:

Co-creation . . . (like end-user generated content) is a recent addition to the knowledge cycle. The ability to build on/with the work of others opens doors for innovation and rapid development of ideas and concepts.

Dissemination . . . (analysis, evaluation, and filtering elements through the network) is the next stage in the knowledge-flow cycle

Communication of key ideas . . . (those that have survived the dissemination process) enter conduits for dispersion throughout the network

Personalization . . . at this stage, we bring new knowledge to ourselves through the experience of internalization, dialogue, or reflection.

Implementation . . . is the final stage, where action occurs and feeds back into the personalization stage. Our understanding of a concept changes when we are acting on it, versus only theorizing or learning about it.

(It is worth noting, even the diagram provided to support this line of reasoning falls into static, almost hierarchical representations—our text/visual tools perpetuate and feed our linearity—a concept we will explore in greater detail when discussing the changed attributes of knowledge).

A simple example is the process of communicating via text. Traditionally, a book was the created knowledge object. Once written, it was released for others to read and disseminate. As an object, the flow of discussion was essentially one way—from the author to the reader (though readers may form book clubs to discuss the work of an author). The original source was not updated regularly, perhaps only in subsequent editions occurring every several years.

In today's online world, an author can post a series of ideas/writings, and receive critique from colleagues, members of other disciplines, or peers from around the world. The ideas can be used by others to build more elaborate (or personalized) representations. The dialogue continues, and ideas gain momentum as they are analyzed and co-created in different variations. After only a brief time (sometimes a matter of days), the ideas can be sharpened, enlarged, challenged, or propagated. The cycle is dizzying in pace, process, and final product, which is then fed back into the flow cycle for continual iteration.

We do not consume knowledge as a passive entity that remains unchanged as it moves through our world and our work. We dance and court the knowledge of others—in ways the original creators did not intend. We make it ours, and in so doing, diminish the prominence of the originator.

Many processes tug at and work the fabric of knowledge.

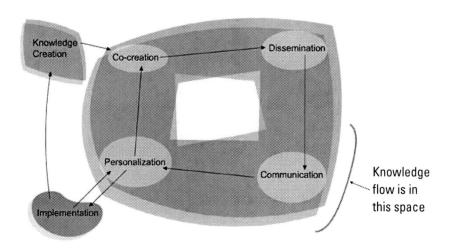

Figure 3. Knowledge Flow Cycle

Rather, knowledge comes to us through

a network of

prejudices,

opinions,

innervations,

self-corrections,

presuppositions

and exaggerations,

in short

through the dense, firmly-founded but by no means

uniformly transparent medium of experience. (Theodor Adorno)[14]

We exist in multiple domains[15]

PHYSICAL   COGNITIVE
EMOTIONAL   SPIRITUAL

It is to our own ill that we consider any one domain above the others. We are most alive, most human, and most complete when we see the full color of our multi-domain continuums.

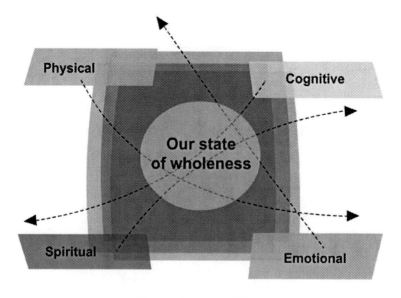

Figure 4. Domains of Knowing

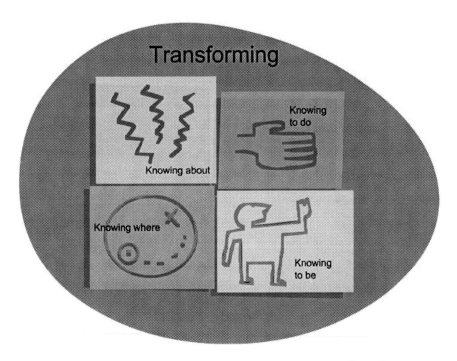

Figure 5.
Knowledge Types

Our quadratic existence runs
through spheres of interconnection.
Cognitive, emotional, physical, and
spiritual domains of knowledge
interact in a myriad of ways.
Life is not lived in a silo.
Artificial constructs may
be useful for categorization,
but fail to capture the true richness
and interconnectivity of knowledge.
The aggregate of domains,
each with various levels
of prominence in different
situations, provides the conduit
through which we experience
knowledge.

KNOWLEDGE consists of different types:

Knowing ABOUT . . . .news events, basics of a field, introductory concepts in a discipline

Knowing TO DO . . . .drive a car, solve a math problem, code a program, conduct research, manage a project

Knowing TO BE . . . .to embody knowledge with humanity (doing blended with consistency and daily existence), to be a doctor or psychologist (mannerism, profession-alism), to be an ethical person, to be compassionate, to relate, to feel

Knowing WHERE . . . .to find knowledge when needed, web search, library, database, an org-anization, and increasingly, knowing who to approach for assistance

Knowing TO TRANSFORM . . . .to tweak, to adjust, to recombine, to align with reality, to innovate, to exist at levels deeper than readily noticeable, to think. The "why of knowing" resides in this domain

We have created journals, books, libraries, and museums to house knowledge. Most knowledge in these storage structures is in the about and doing levels. Knowing to be, where to find knowledge (in today's environment, knowing how to navigate knowledge as a process or flow), and knowing to transform are all outside of these container-views.

Schools, universities, and corporations attempt to serve dissemination processes of knowledge-in-containers. Under the pressure of constant, ongoing change (and being designed to manage products not processes), these organizations are unable to attend to the full array of knowing. For most of us, we find our higher-level understanding through reflection and informal learning, where we engage with knowledge to gain new understandings. The skills and processes that will make us people of tomorrow are not yet embedded in our educational structures. While there are many who are attempting new approaches, the vast majority are ensconced in structures, preparing students and employees for a future that will not exist.

The quad-space of self occurs in the larger space of organizations and society; just as we exist in different domains: physical, cognitive, social, and spiritual (see Figure 4), we exist in different spaces: self, collective, organizational, and societal (see Figure 6).

Each space of existence holds its own culture. Knowledge experienced in the space of self holds a different context (and thereby, meaning) than knowledge experienced in our collective spaces (hobbies, volunteer groups, social spaces). Each sphere of existence has an accompanying culture and feel (an evolving zeitgeist)…which, themselves, become perspective-points for perceiving (and filtering) knowledge.

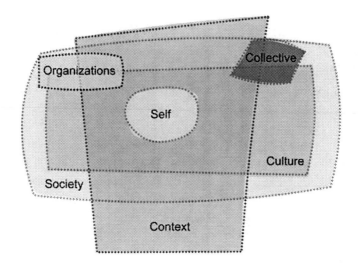

Figure 6. Our Structures of Existence

The complexities of functioning in numerous (and ambiguous) spaces requires increased lines of communication. Duncan Watts addresses the challenge of rapidly changing environments through "intense communication," ensuring that each agent in the space is aware and informed.

> When solving complex problems in ambiguous environments,
> individuals compensate for their limited knowledge of
> the interdependencies between their various tasks and for their
> uncertainty about the future by exchanging information—
> knowledge, advice, expertise, and resources—
> with other problem-solvers within the same organization.
>
> Duncan Watts[16]

An important scientific innovation rarely makes its way by by gradually winning over and converting its opponents. It rarely happens that Saul becomes Paul. What does happen is its opponents gradually die out and the growing generation is familiarized with the idea from the beginning.

Max Planck[17]

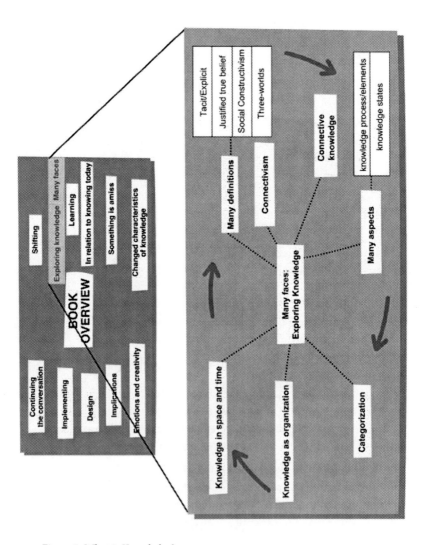

Figure 7. What is Knowledge?

In order to understand beauty, we kill it.

And in the process,

we understand more about our nature

and less about beauty.

MANY FACES
Exploring Knowledge

*The categories of human thought are never fixed
in any one definite form; they are made, unmade and
remade incessantly; they change with places and times.*

Emile Durkheim[18]

Understanding knowledge in a particular era is important in ensuring
that we have aligned our spaces and structures with the nature of
knowledge. Until recently, we have been able to make knowledge fit our
models. Now that we are entering a two-way flow model, (where original sources receive feedback from end-users) we need to adjust our
models to fit the changed nature of *"what it means to know."*

As promised in the preface, this book is not intended to provide a
definition of knowledge. Rather, the intent is to present characteristics
we may consider in exploring the richness of the landscape. A hiker
entering a new territory would think it foolish to settle on a simple,
myopic, diluted definition of the ecology. Instead, the rich space is
explored for plant and animal life, streams and lakes; sounds and smells.
Any singular definition of the landscape would fail to define the whole.
Each definition of the landscape becomes valuable when it abandons
pretences of being the only one and acknowledges other perceptions.
This does not embrace relativity (in each context, one view may be the
most appropriate. Paul Boghossian, in his exploration of truth, belief,
and facts, rejects the notion that "all views are equally valid"[19]). It does,
however, embrace diversity, acknowledging that many different views
exist, and different ones will be more applicable in different situations
(each context may better align with one particular view, eliminating the
notion of equal validity of all views in a particular context).

Many have provided knowledge definitions and models:

- Justified true belief (Socrates and Plato);
- A gradient of data, information, knowledge, understanding, and wisdom; [20]
- Defined by tacit and explicit spirals: socialization (tacit to tacit), externalization (tacit to explicit), combination (explicit to explicit), and internalization (explicit to tacit);[21]
- Three worlds of knowledge: one–physical/material, two–physiological/ subjective, and three–culture/artifacts;[22]
- Sense-making and organization.[23]

Can multiple definitions of knowledge be true?

Can knowledge exist independent of **human** knowing?

Is knowledge ACQUIRED or is it CREATED through active participation?

Is knowledge a personal activity? Do we socially construct knowledge?

The aim of argument, or of discussion, should not be victory, but progress.
Joseph Joupert[24]

Knowledge can be described in many ways; an entity and a process, a sequence of continuums: type, level, and application, implicit, explicit, tacit, procedural, declarative, inductive, deductive, qualitative, and quantitative. Knowledge **rests** in an individual; it **resides** in the collective.

While not ascribing to pure subjectivity views of knowledge (some things are, and we must align ourselves with them—pure subjectivity is the playground of theorists and philosophers. Reality often presents both objective and subjective elements[25]), we can see that certain things may be appropriate in one context, while not in another.

Knowledge in the pharmaceutical field will possess different traits than knowledge in agriculture. Different definitions will apply based on different understandings. A knowledge product (a mathematical formula) is different from a knowledge process (ongoing attempt to stay current in a world of accelerating knowledge). To see in monochromatic views is to fail to see the full breadth of knowledge.

We must become skilled at seeing continuums and context.

We may periodically ascribe object-like elements to knowledge, but only for the ability to discuss, debate, and dialogue. For example, research in neuroscience reveals patterns that can be presented and shared with other researchers. The moment, however, that knowledge is created, it becomes subject to the knowledge flow cycle discussed previously...where knowledge leads to co-creation, dissemination, communication, personalization, implementation, and ongoing cycles of building and sharing.

Today we may be able to say that "the brain works this way," but only if we acknowledge that the discoveries themselves are emerging. We are constantly expanding our understanding (revisiting our preconceived notions) and forcing the brain to reveal its functioning. Our understanding is a transitory state, influenced by our domains of knowing (see Figure 4): cognitive, emotional, physical, and spiritual, and types of knowledge (see Figure 5): about, to do, to be, know where, and transforming, as well as our structures of existence (see Figure 6): self, collective, organizational, and societal.

Social tools are emerging which permit rapid exchange of knowledge, and high levels of dialogue. Communication can now occur collaboratively (wiki, online meetings), through individual broadcast (blogs, podcasts, video logs), and in shared spaces (social bookmarking). Knowledge, when buffeted by numerous forces and factors, is under constant scrutiny by the masses.

Perhaps we should pursue a therapy view of knowledge. Therapies create understanding only after all elements (which are constantly changing) have been considered. We must resist the urge to give shape too early. Ambiguity is an unfailing companion. Constructs, and classifications represent only part of the knowledge space—primarily those knowledge elements that have hardened (see Figure 8).

In a broad sense, knowledge has historically been defined or categorized along two lines: quantitative or qualitative. We require an epistemology that subsumes or, at minimum, extends these viewpoints into our world today.

Knowing and learning are today defined by connections. CONNECTIVISM[26] is the assertion that learning is primarily a network-forming process.

Downes provides connective knowledge[27] as the epistemological foundation of connectivism:

A property of one entity must lead to or become a property of another entity in order for them to be considered connected; the knowledge that results from such connections is connective knowledge.

Connective knowledge networks possess four traits:

DIVERSITY. . . . Is the widest possible spectrum of points of view revealed?

AUTONOMY. . . . Were the individual knowers contributing to the interaction of their own accord, according to their own knowledge, values and decisions, or were they acting at the behest of some external agency seeking to magnify a certain point of view through quantity rather than reason and reflection?

INTERACTIVITY. . . . Is the knowledge being produced the product of an interaction between the members, or is it a (mere) aggregation of the members' perspectives?

OPENNESS. . . . Is there a mechanism that allows a given perspective to be entered into the system, to be heard and interacted with by others?

We must negotiate knowledge definitions, as a doctor provides therapy for a patient. Our knowledge definitions and activities are dances of context (or, to abuse Wittgenstein[28], much of the process of knowledge is a context game). We may encounter situations where tacit and explicit views serve our purposes…or where justified true belief is an appropriate definition. Context and purpose often reveal the *needed* definition (not the definition formulated in advance and applied to different situations).

The context game should reveal the nature of knowledge in each space. Some things *are,* and we are most effective when we align to *what is*[29]. In other instances, the nature of knowledge is vague, ambiguous, or chaotic. Our treatment and approach must be defined by the nature of knowledge we are considering.

To arrive at a true definition of knowledge is to render it useless for diverse implementation.

A broad definition is possible (much like we can ascribe broad characteristics to mammals), and while the specific functions in the larger whole, we must see each knowledge element/experience/interaction for what it uniquely is (like we ascribe certain characteristics to dogs, or cats…and further provide detailed breakdown of species and types). The more precise the definition, the less applicable in multiple situations.

If a financial services organization is seeking to improve the ability of employees to provide rapid loan approvals, the needed knowledge cannot be defined in advance. Decisions are made based on multiple factors—each carrying a different weight in the final outcome. The supporting processes, which allow employees quick access to needed knowledge—credit rating, debt ratios in different sectors, enable and foster decision making. Access to knowledge is not enough—the mark of complex functioning is the following of a few simple rules.[30] Instead of defining the construct of knowledge and decision-making, simple rules, guided by access to needed knowledge, permit individuals to make complex decisions.

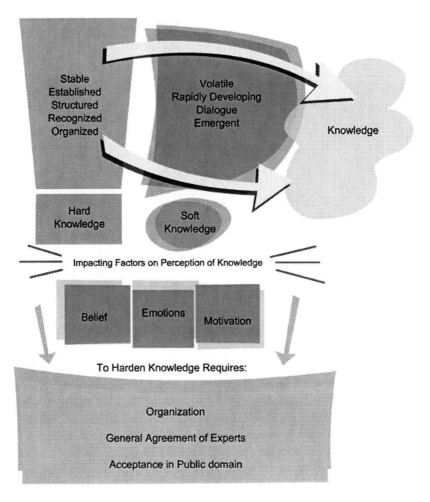

Figure 8. Knowledge States

Knowledge possesses different states…along a continuum. Hard knowledge occurs in fields and eras where change is slow. Through a process of expert validation and acceptance of the public, knowledge acquires solid states. Over the last several decades, more of our knowledge has shifted to soft knowledge. When things change rapidly, many knowledge elements do not have time to harden before they are replaced or amended. Managing hard and soft knowledge (as a continuum, not distinct points) requires different processes.

We have a different relationship with knowledge that has been *crystallized* in the form of a book or a journal. Why do we respect it more?

Do increased input costs of time or finances equate with increased value? Do copyright and ownership claims raise value?

Knowledge is subject to numerous processes (see Figure 9)—how it is created; by experts or the masses, structured; in preset containers or clouds and networks of nebulous shape, disseminated; one-way models like books or journals or soft two-way flow of the internet, validated; by experts or peers, and acquired and implemented; through content consumption, dialogue, or reflection.

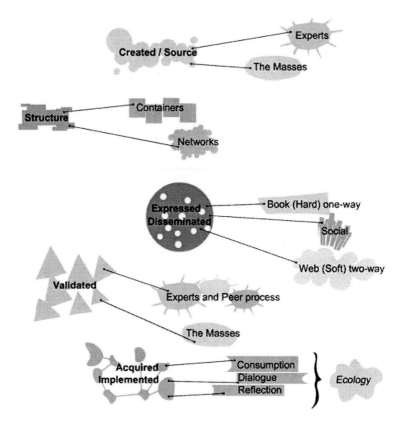

Figure 9. Knowledge Process/Elements

Each of these processes is currently being reshaped and changed as knowledge changes. Technology is providing new affordances for individuals to become involved in publishing, knowledge exchange, and to access experts.

Definitions are subject to numerous elements that reduce their effectiveness: language and meaning, context, culture, and perspective. We cannot define a field by one definition. Instead, definitions need to be created on a one-to-one basis. Explore the entity. Then decide. Do not force the entity into preformed containers.

Organizationally, our challenge is to *work with knowledge based on its characteristics, not on our pre-created viewpoints.* We need to resist the urge "to make something "familiar" even at the cost of destroying what [we have] found."[31] We can no longer create our filters in advance. We must learn to dance (engage and interact) with knowledge in order to understand what it is.

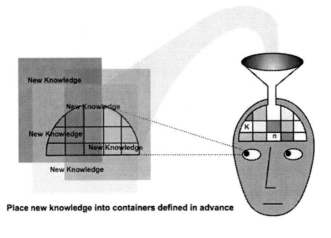

Place new knowledge into containers defined in advance

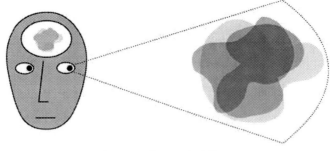

Permit knowledge to emerge based on "What it is"

Figure 10. Categorization

Knowledge is organization. **NOT STRUCTURE.**

KNOWLEDGE IS NOT INTENDED TO FILL MINDS. IT IS INTENDED TO OPEN THEM.

Traditional knowledge organization consisted of fairly static hierarchies and containers. Organization today consists of dynamic networks and ecologies—models capable of adaptation (adjusting and reacting to changes). Structure is the outgrowth of organization, not the pre-requisite to organization.

What we define as knowledge is the codification of information or data in a particular way. The principles of gravity existed long before they were articulated in a manner that could be communicated, analyzed, and explored. Seeing the pattern (how things were organized and what that organization meant), is the resulting knowledge.

Similarly, the ability to perform a heart transplant existed as a theory before actual doing in reality. The knowledge to build the machines, procedures, and accompanying elements resulted from a particular recombination of information.

Our cognitive efforts are not exclusively structured and hierarchical. We explore information with a desire to personalize and *patternize—* to translate into knowledge.

Figure 11 presents elements involved in the knowledge process:

- Knowledge seeker   • Content   • Context
- Conduits (the medium through which knower and seeker communicate…and through which the known entity finds expression)
- Knower/Expert

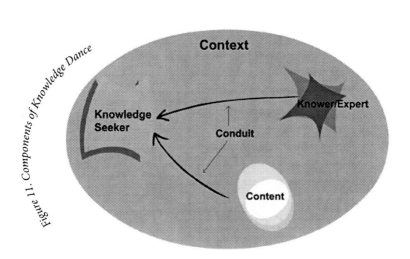

Figure 11. Components of Knowledge Dance

Knowledge comes from systems and integrated structures. Better quality networks and connections result in better quality knowledge sharing. Forming effective networks is as important a challenge as utilizing the networks for our knowledge needs.

While building our networks, we cannot unearth knowledge by only focusing on one domain. To exclude social, emotional, or spiritual dimensions is to grey the picture. The wider the lens of our perception, the brighter (and more complete) the image.

What are trusted sources of knowledge?

What skills and processes do we need to work with soft knowledge (see Figure 8)? We have spent our history with hard/codified knowledge as a product. We now need to learn to work with soft knowledge as a process.

How does it happen today? How is knowledge vetted for validity and authenticity? The opinions and views of experts are augmented by trusted networks (like recommender systems in many communities—to validate individuals based on their history and previous activities within a space). Checks and balances, not hierarchical structures, create vetting models.

Can a group be as effective as an expert?

We experience knowledge in time and space allowing us to see from only one point at a time (we cannot hold opposing perspectives, even though we are aware of others).

A network reflects on itself. I am a node on my own network. I can only see and think from where I exist. If I move, I lose the initial perspective. We cannot maintain two points in our network simultaneously. Understanding that a different view exists is very different from seeing the different view.

Learning is the equivalent of opening a door to a new way of perceiving and knowing. An open door leads to corridors of new thought and ways of knowing (or forgetting).

WE EXPERIENCE KNOWLEDGE IN TIME AND SPACE.

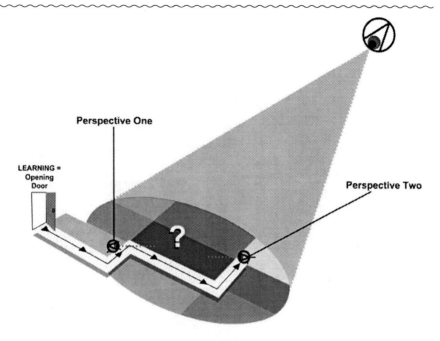

Figure 12. Time and Space

The newspaper editor, the news station, the radio host, who is able to promote and filter based on certain viewpoints (political, philosophical), is losing ground to the individual. Individuals can form and create their own spaces and networks of news, information, and knowledge filtering and dissemination.

We do not live our lives in active cognition. We spend much of our time in containers that we have created. Instead of thinking, we are merely sorting and filtering. (Or has sorting become the thinking of our era?). Even user-created networks resist active cognition in order to filter out contrasting viewpoints. The new spaces of knowledge, while conceptually democratic, are subject to the same quest for certainty and consistency that we desire in other knowledge sources. Wikipedia, an online encyclopedia written by numerous contributors, (not necessarily experts as traditional encyclopedias require), still requires certainty and validity. Wikipedia requires structure and control—though of a different nature. Instead of command and control models, guidelines are created through dialogue and transparency.

Our containers of organization are cracking. We are entering a new stage of active, ongoing cognition. We can no longer rely on categorization to meet our needs in a rapidly evolving, global knowledge climate. We must rely on network-formation and development of knowledge ecologies. We must become different people with different habits.

Figure 13. Learning

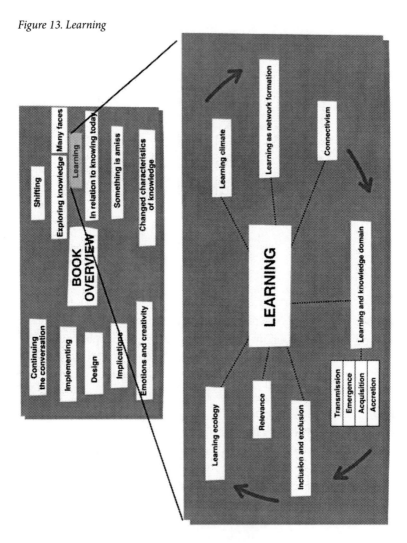

  ❝At the end of the last century, knowledge began to become the most valuable currency, like land in a feudal economy or capital in an industrial economy. The new science of learning should tell us that knowledge is not just a prize to be won in some desperate test-taking struggle for places in the contemporary mandarinate. Instead it is, literally and not just rhetorically, our universal human birthright. ❞
J. Brockman[32]

LEARNING

The future of learning is written in the future of knowledge.
Stephen Downes[33]

Mass education designed for the industrial age meets the needs of neither the pre-industrial village nor the post-industrial future... indeed, all education—has to be totally reconceptualised.
Alvin Toffler[34]

In *Educating the Net Generation*[35] Diana and James Oblinger present an example of today's youth—influenced and changed by technology. Eric (the individual in their introduction), lives a different reality—not because *of* technology, but because of affordances provided *by* technology. For Eric, connecting with people and content is a constant, ongoing, daily activity. His learning is a continual, network-forming process. This model is gaining prominence in both academic and corporate environments. As we encounter new resources (knowledge, people, and technology nodes), we may choose to actively connect and create our personal learning network.

Learning is more than knowledge acquisition. Often it is a process of several stages with several distinct components. Exploration, inquiry, decision making, selecting, and deselecting are all preparatory activities before we even enter the learning experience (the learning experience being defined as the moment when we actively acquire the knowledge that is missing in order for us to complete the needed tasks or solve a problem).

During (and following) the learning experience, evaluations and assessments are occurring that measure if the learning needed has occurred. Each stage has different requirements. Preparatory learning relies more on informal tools; the learning experience most likely utilizes structured content and dialogue with gurus; the evaluation stage requires informal discussion, reflection, and self-expression. One tool or approach does not adequately address the entire process.

We need to ensure that we do not talk about learning in its entirety when we are really only referring to a certain stage or a certain type of learning. For example, if I was to say "learning communities are great for learning," but fail to specify that I am referring to the preparatory stage of learning in order to foster innovation, my ambiguity makes it difficult to dialogue with others on the concept (we will address this phenomena as context games in the next chapter). The listener may have a different focus of a particular learning stage or learning type and will attempt to engage/refute my comments from her/his own perspective.

We end up talking past each other. When we talk learning, we need to state the stage, the type, and the process to which we are referring. This discussion is similar to the knowledge discussion presented in the first two sections of this book. Defining the entity itself, not implementing our pre-defined processes, is critical.

Learning is a peer to knowledge. To learn is to come to know. To know is to have learned. We seek knowledge so that we can make sense. Knowledge today requires a shift from cognitive processing to pattern recognition.

Our metaphors of thought over the last century include:

> Our mind is a **BLACK BOX** . . .We can not fully know what goes on. Instead, we focus on the behavior— the observable manifestation of thought and cognition.
>
> Our mind is like a **COMPUTER** . . .We accept inputs, manage them in short-term memory, archive them in long-term memory (and retrieve into short-term memory when needed), generating some type of output.
>
> Our mind constructs our **REALITY** . . .We engage in active construction of our reality through the ideas and resources we encounter.

These established metaphors fall short in an era defined by rapid knowledge development. Our mind is not like a computer. Neuroscience has revealed that the computer model is wholly inaccurate. Our mind may have been a black box to researchers a century ago, but we now understand many of the functions of different areas of our brain...

we are slowly illuminating the box. Construction, while a useful metaphor, fails to align with our growing understanding that our mind is a connection-creating structure. We do not always construct (which is high cognitive load), but we do constantly connect.

We need to break false modes of thinking in relation to knowledge.

> ## Our mind is a network…an ecology.
> ## It adapts to the environment.

We cannot think of new directions while we are in battle with the boundaries of existing thought and context. Our thoughts exist in time and space (as neural points in an integrated network).

How we create corporate policies (how we design our knowledge flows) should be in line with how we learn and think. Cold logic does not serve an organization well. Neither does untamed emotion.

Holistic, multi-faceted views of learning, knowledge, corporate activities are required. Gain diverse perspectives…test/pilot/experiment… nurture…select…and amplify. Meyer and Davis reduce the concept even further:

> *Seed, Select, and Amplify. Test many diverse options, and reinforce the winners. Experiment, don't plan.*
>
> *Chris Meyer and Stan Davis*[36]

LEARNING (see Figure 14) is defined by:

CHAOTIC
Diverse and messy, not necessarily neatly packaged and arranged.

CONTINUAL
Ongoing in development and communication. The model of "go to a course" is being replaced with learning and knowledge at the point of need.

CO-CREATION
Instead of content consumption (or passive learners involved in knowledge acquisition), experts and amateurs are now co-creators in knowledge.

COMPLEXITY
Learning is a multi-faceted, integrated process where changes with any one element alters the larger network. Knowledge is subject to the nuances of complex, adaptive systems.

CONNECTED SPECIALIZATION

Complexity and diversity results in specialized nodes (a single entity can no longer know all required elements). The act of knowledge growth and learning involves connected specialized nodes

CONTINUAL SUSPENDED CERTAINTY

We know in part. An attitude of tolerance for ambiguity and uncertainty is required. Certainty is for a season, not a lifetime.

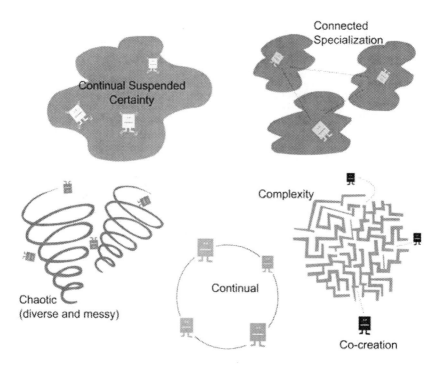

Figure 14. Traits of Learning Today

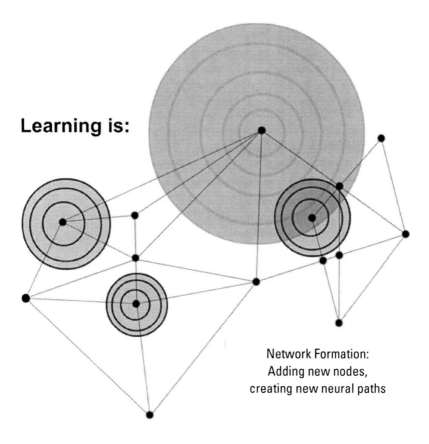

Learning is:

Network Formation:
Adding new nodes,
creating new neural paths

Figure 15. Learning as Network Forming

Learning is the process of creating networks. Nodes are external entities which we can use to form a network. Or nodes may be people, organizations, libraries, web sites, books, journals, database, or any other source of information. The act of learning (things become a bit tricky here) is one of creating an *external network* of nodes—where we connect and form information and knowledge sources. The learning that happens in our heads is an *internal network (neural)*. Learning networks can then be perceived as structures that we create in order to stay current and continually acquire, experience, create, and connect new knowledge (external). And learning networks can be perceived as structures that exist within our minds (internal) in connecting and creating patterns of understanding.

Not all nodes within a learning network continue to remain relevant. As an intelligent network, our mind continually reshapes and adjusts to reflect new environments and information. Corporations undergo a similar process. Nodes that are no longer valued are *weakened* within this environment.

Weakening can occur in many ways, but the most obvious is a loss of connections within the network. For example, if I believe in the Loch Ness monster, this belief can exist as an unobtrusive node because it does not generally impact my daily activities. As a result, the node is largely ignored (information and ideas are not routed through this node). As I encounter new sources of information critical of the concept of the Loch Ness monster, I may eventually weaken the node sufficiently to eliminate its relevance in my neural network.

A learner who continually encounters new information and knowledge, will dynamically update and rewrite his/her network of learning and belief. If on the other hand, the node itself is critical (that is, it is a hub or is heavily connected), weakening will only happen over a long period of time or through seismic shifts across the entire network. Such cross-network shifts assume that the emotional nodes, which route information critical of beliefs, permit fluidity of new ideas, instead of simply using new information through the perspective of existing beliefs.

Connectivism is a theory describing how learning happens in a digital age. Research in traditional learning theories comes from an era when net-working technologies were not yet prominent. How does learning change when knowledge growth is overwhelming and technology replaces many basic tasks we have previously performed?

Connectivism is the integration of principles explored by chaos[37], network, complexity[38], and self-organization[39] theories.

Knowledge and learning are processes that occur within nebulous environments of shifting core elements—not entirely under the control of the individual. Learning (defined as knowledge patterns on which we can act) can reside outside of ourselves (within an organization or a database), is focused on connecting specialized information sets. *The connections that enable us to learn more are more important than our current state of knowing.*

Connectivism is driven by the understanding that decisions are based on rapidly altering foundations.

New knowledge is continually being acquired. Drawing distinctions between important and unimportant knowledge is vital. The ability to recognize when new knowledge alters the landscape based on decisions made yesterday is important. When business, or academic, environments change, adjustments need to be made in our own thinking and assumptions to ensure that we are basing our decisions on an accurate foundation.

PRINCIPLES OF CONNECTIVISM:

- Learning and knowledge require diversity of opinions to present the whole…and to permit selection of best approach.
- Learning is a network formation process of connecting specialized nodes or information sources.
- Knowledge rests in networks.
- Knowledge may reside in non-human appliances , and learning is enabled/facilitated by technology.[40]
- Capacity to know more is more critical than what is currently known.
- Learning and knowing are constant, on going processes (not end states or products).
- Ability to see connections and recognize patterns and make sense between fields, ideas, and concepts is the core skill for individuals today.
- Currency (accurate, up-to-date knowledge) is the intent of all connectivist learning activities.
- Decision-making is learning. Choosing what to learn and the meaning of incoming information is seen through the lens of a shifting reality. While there is a right answer now, it may be wrong tomorrow due to alterations in the information climate affecting the decision.

> By obsolete, I mean that our high schools–
> even when they're working exactly as designed–
> cannot teach our kids what they need to know today ….
> Training the workforce of tomorrow with the high schools
> of today is like trying to teach kids about today's computers
> on a 50-year-old mainframe. It's the wrong tool for the times.
>
> Bill Gates[41]

"Know where" and "know who" are more important today that knowing what and how. An information rich world requires the ability to first determine what is important, and then how to stay connected and informed as information changes. Content is dependant on the right conduit for expression and communication (the internet, a book, a text message, an email, a short video clip).

Learners in a physical space should strive to enrich their own network with online tools and resources. Network creation enables learners to continue to stay current in the face of rapidly developing knowledge. The pipe is more important than the content within the pipe (simply because content changes rapidly).

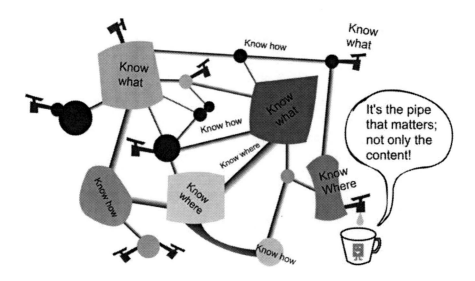

Figure 16. Know Where

Knowledge is of two kinds: we know a subject ourselves,
or we know where we can find information upon it.

Samuel Johnson[42]

Our changing knowledge and learning contexts are axiomatic. We see it in many forms—from newspapers to radio to TV to the internet. Everything is going digital. The end user is gaining control, elements are decentralizing, connections are being formed between formerly disparate resources and fields of information, and everything seems to be *speeding up.*

The Achilles heel of existing theories rests in the pace of knowledge growth. All existing theories place processing (or interpretation) of knowledge on the individual doing the learning. This model works well if the knowledge flow is moderate. A constructivist view of learning, for example, suggests that we process, interpret, and derive personal meaning from different information formats. What happens, however, when knowledge is more of a deluge than a trickle? What happens when knowledge flows too fast for processing or interpreting?

Once flow becomes too rapid and complex, we need a model that allows individuals to learn and function in spite of the pace and flow. A network model of learning (an attribute of connectivism) offloads some of the processing and interpreting functions of knowledge flow to nodes within a learning network. Instead of the individual having to evaluate and process every piece of information, she/he creates a personal network of trusted nodes: people and content, enhanced by technology. The learner aggregates relevant nodes...and relies on each individual node to provide needed knowledge. The act of knowing is offloaded onto the network itself. This view of learning scales well with continued complexity and pace of knowledge development.

A simple example: the age of solitary skilled professionals is giving way to team-based functioning. The increased complexity of our world today does not permit any one individual an accurate understanding of the entire scope of a situation, field, or subject. We now rely on connected specialization—where we increase our competence by adding specialized functionality to our network. Building an airplane, performing a complicated surgery, or analyzing foreign market trends are involved tasks that require knowledge to be offloaded to a connected network of specialists. No one individual has the competence to build an airplane, perform an involved surgery, or comprehend market trends. The network (or web) of connections is the structure which holds the knowledge of individuals in a holistic manner.

We forage for knowledge—we keep looking until we find people, tools, content, and processes that assist us in solving problems. Our natural capacity for learning is tremendous. We overcome many obstacles and restrictions to achieve our goals. The problem rests largely in the view that learning is a managed process, not a fostered process. When learning is seen as a function of an ecology, diverse options and opportunities are required.

Learning has many dimensions. No one model or definition will fit every situation. **CONTEXT IS CENTRAL.**

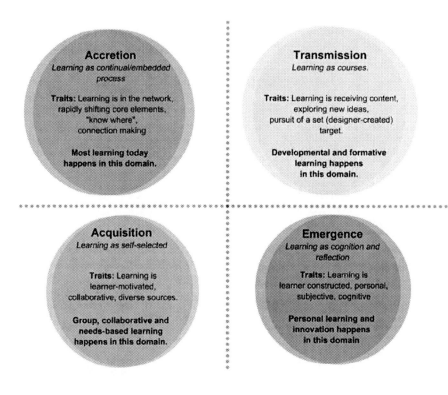

Figure 17. Learning and Knowledge Domains[43]

Transmission Learning is based on traditional views. The learner is brought into a system, and through lectures and courses, is exposed to structured knowledge. This domain is useful for building core knowledge elements of a field or discipline. The model, however, is expensive to implement (one instructor, twenty students) and is at odds with how much of our learning happens (social, two-way, ongoing).

Emergence Learning involves greater emphasis on the learner's cognition and reflection. The learner acquires and creates (or at minimum, internalizes) knowledge. This domain is effective for *deep learning,* and can foster innovation and higher-level cognition. The model is hard to implement large scale, as it requires competence and critical thinking in each learner, as well as high familiarity with the subject matter.

The **Acquisition Domain** of learning is exploratory and inquiry-based. The learner is in control of defining the needed knowledge, and actively enters the process in order to assuage personal motivations and interests. Pure self-directed learning can be a concern in some organizations, especially when the learner is expected to meet clear, defined outcomes. Too often, lack of structure is equated with lack of focus. Self-directed learning (which is often the bulk of our learning—we are constantly pursuing subject matter and knowledge which is of personal interest or related to our competence in our work places) is viewed as being too loose.[44]

The fourth domain, **Accretion Learning,** is continuous. As a function of the environment, the learner forages for knowledge when and where it is needed. Real life, not theory, drives this learning type. As an ongoing, natural process, learners and organizations are apt to devalue or deem-phasize accretion learning. Accretion learning is the constant activity of our work and life. We gain new insights from conversations, from a workshop, or an article. We gain experience through our reflection on failed (or successful) projects. We connect and bring together numerous elements and activities, constantly shaping and creating our understanding and knowledge.

In learning, we usually focus on what we are including in our reasoning (learning and knowledge acquisition are often seen as similar concepts). We generally associate learning with gaining something. There is value in determining the role of exclusion in learning. What we choose to exclude in order to learn may provide as much information as what we actually include.

> Even revolutionaries conserve; all cultures are conservative.
> This is so because it is a systemic phenomenon:
> all systems exist only as long as there is conservation
> of that which defines them.
> Humberto Maturana Romesin & Pille Bunnell[45]

Learning filters through some type of framework. This framework is an aggregation of personal beliefs, networks, experiences, existing knowledge, and emotional intelligence. As an example, (if we can briefly utilize stereotypes for illustration purposes) conservatives are usually perceived as business focused, whereas liberals are perceived as people (or social issue) focused. These political worldviews shape and influence the type of information that penetrates into our active region of thinking and deliberation.

Often, we exclude from thought those concepts which are strongly antagonistic to views we already hold. Back to the stereotypes of conservatives/liberals—when these two groups engage in dialogue, they are largely speaking past each other. Instead of embracing each other in an attempt to understand what is really being said, the debate centers on what each party has *included* in their thinking...while focusing on what the other party has *excluded* in their thinking.

The conservative promotes the value of business, the liberal the value of social structures. The conservative criticizes the liberal's lack of business focus; the liberal criticizes the conservative's lack of social focus. *We argue our points of inclusion and criticize the points of exclusion in the reasoning of others.* Similarly, we are uniquely susceptible to logical fallacies in domains in which we have strong beliefs.[46] The stronger our beliefs, the more susceptible we are to fallacies.

The process of exclusion is a vital learning process. We cannot possibly consider every facet of a new idea. We exclude in order to move to the point of active cognition on, or interaction with, an idea. Exclusion occurs during the filtering process. What we choose to ignore speaks to our larger worldview (beliefs and values). When we are trying to influence the values of others (for example, in helping students learn about other cultures), we spend our time trying to get the learner to acquire new mindsets.

By analyzing what we exclude in our own reasoning, we are able to gain a better understand of our own learning process. It is unrealistic to regularly evaluate our core beliefs and values, but a periodic evaluation may provide the ability for more effective learning in general. What we ignore in learning can be a valuable tool to ensure that our perspectives are properly balanced (and, at minimum, acknowledge the existence of viewpoints contrary to our own). Sometimes, the ability to step out of our thought corridor, and into a different corridor, can lead to deep insight and understanding. Not all learning (or cognitive activity) is logical. The choice to include/exclude information may be the point where emotional intelligence (how we handle ourselves and our relationships[47]) exerts its greatest influence.

RELEVANCE is THE requirement for adoption or use of virtually anything. If something is not relevant, it is not used (this can be a concern when we overlook knowledge that is not relevant today, but may be a key element in developing our competence tomorrow).

RELEVANCE can best be defined as the degree to which a resource or activity matches an individual's needs. The closer the match, the greater the potential value.

What then does it mean for knowledge to be relevant?
Is it a function of being current?
Or tightly linked to the task at hand?

A learner must be able to see relevance. If relevance (determined by the individual) is not ascertained, motivation will not be enacted. Lack of motivation results in lack of action.

Relevance, however, is not only about the nature of content. The process of ensuring currency of content/information is critical—to manage knowledge growth and function effectively in a diminishing half-life of knowledge environment.

Some institutions are beginning to explore alternative models of content delivery—for learning and sharing knowledge. Elearning initially focused on simply duplicating classroom activities, so content was generally created in linear, course-sized chunks. In order to learn, an individual needed to devote a large amount of time to exploring content. Alteration in size, manner, and point of content delivery (rather than a course, learning can be delivered in smaller, individual objectives...in a variety of formats—computer, paper-based, cell phone) enables knowledge to be expressed continuously, rather than in structured courses. The content needs to be *findable* at the learner's point of need, as compared to learning being provided *just-in-case.*

The more closely the content is positioned to the point of doing/need, the more effective the learning process. Additionally, it is important to acknowledge that learning is much more than exposure to content. Social, community, and collaborative approaches to learning are important.

The second criteria for relevance in today's environment is for institutions to ensure that content is current. This is a significant challenge. By nature, a course or training is prepared months in advance of delivery, and is then modified as needed based on new information. Courses are fairly static. Knowledge is dynamic—changing hourly, daily. Content designers require an understanding of the nature of the half-life of knowledge in their field and ensure that they select the right tools to keep content current for the learners.

Admittedly, currency of content requires far more thinking and planning than described here. Content management systems, aggregators, intelligent search, and other tools are part of the overall structure of ensuring content is up to date. Current learning formats are antagonistic to the evolving nature of knowledge. We need to augment our view of what it means to be current in our fields...and how we propose to tap learners into a larger structure that continues to provide value well beyond the close of a course.

Our organizational views of knowledge need to be expanded. Knowledge is not only a product–it is also a process. It does not function and flow as physical goods did in the industrial era.

The paths that create knowledge run through valleys of learning. We often equate knowledge acquisition or creation with formal learning. But we find knowledge in many ways: informal learning, experimentation, dialogue, thinking, and reflection.

Learning *happens* as we live life in our current knowledge economy. In fact, information comes at us constantly—TV program, newspaper article, a workshop, or a problem we solve on our own. We incorporate many of these points in how we see the world and how we do our work.

This concept of **networked learning** answers many questions about how we acquire much of our knowledge (even elements that contradict each other). When we exist in a knowledge climate (or network), we constantly scan, evaluate, and select for use, elements that answer questions with which we are struggling. Some elements of learning will relate to our values, attitudes, and beliefs, others will relate more concretely to how we perform our work. In an election season, politicians rely heavily on *teaching* the electorate through a network imbued with their message.

If the electorate is unwilling to accept the message directly, perhaps it will accept the message when embedded in our existing learning network (an unpalatable concept is more attractive when it links, even if inaccurately, to our existing values and lines of reasoning).

The learning system in many organizations is still largely based on the schema that the learner is an empty container that we fill. We talk about dynamic, learner-centered instruction. Often those words deny the reality that our institutions are primarily set up to *fill learners.* We promote empowerment for knowledge workers, yet we expect them to function in a manner at odds with how knowledge is created and how it flows.

What should our structures look like?

OPEN ... anyone able to speak into the process
GOVERNANCE ... by those represented
FOSTERED ... not only structured
CONDUCIVE ... to knowledge flow, with barriers and
obstructions eliminated

Our solution lies in seeing the whole. Monochromatic one-model, one-approach views do not work in complex spaces like learning and knowledge. Shades, continuums, and blurred boundaries are our new reality.

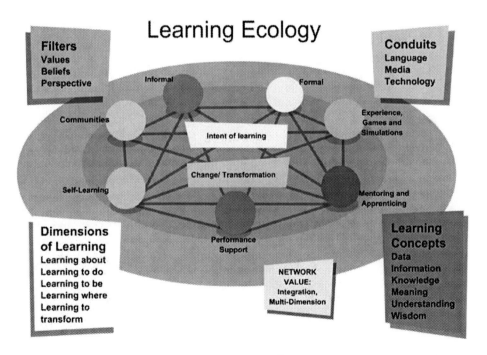

Connectivism: Process of creating network

Figure 18. Learning Ecology

Table 1. **TYPES OF LEARNING IN A LEARNING ECOLOGY**

Tool	For What	Why?	Good for...	Drawbacks..
Formal Learning	Courses Programs Degrees -Defined by established knowledge -Structure imposed by experts in advance of learning	Structure, serve stakeholders, focused	Initiating learners who are new (foundation building)	When learning *at the point of need* is required
Experience/ Game	Problem-Based Learning Ill-defined learning targets User defines process and space Adaptive, flexible	Experiential (learning as a by-product of other activities)	Life Challenges	If foundations are not in place (or the learning experience [as games} needs to provide foundation)
Mentor	Personal Guided and facilitated by *expert*	Accelerate personal performance	Personal, relevant knowledge/ learning	Foundation forming, *high bandwidth*
Performance Support	Learning at the point of need Can rely on other learning approaches	Point of need, competence, assistive	Short, focused learning	Developing foundations of a discipline
Self-learning	Meta-cognition Learning about learning Learning that is personally driven	Learning for pleasure, personal competence	Exploring areas of personal interest	How do learners know what they need to know?
Community-based Learning	Diversity "Wisdom of the crowds" Social/ dialogue	Create multi-faceted view of a space or discipline	Dialogue, diversity of perspective	Foundational *high time requirement*
Informal Learning	Conferences Workshops Colleagues	Serendipity, constant, ongoing, *in the stream*	Continual, ongoing, multifaceted	Chaotic, not always valued, scattered

We often have a mismatch between tool and process. Learning is not a clear, structured, uni-directional process. Learning is messy and chaotic. As a simple analogy, if our main goal is to travel somewhere fast (our intended function/process) and we opt to walk (even when a vehicle is available), we are being foolish (again, assuming that our main goal is fast travel, not environmentalism). In our organizational technology and learning structures, we often give vendors control of learning—due to their control of tool integration. This creates an environment where the tool drives what we are able to do (rather than our learning and communication goals driving the technology). Universities, colleges, and corporations often use learning management or e-portfolio systems. The functionality (how employees and students will learn) is driven by the tool selected. Where we desire multiple options, the tool often presents limited functionality. Too often, we bend our pedagogy to the tool.

It is not about **controlling**. It is about **fostering**…and **guiding**.

Fostering learning requires rethinking the tools used. Do the tools work in the manner in which people learn? Who has control of the tools? Who benefits most from implementation of the tools (administrators, educators, learners)? What are the metrics of success (return on investment, learning)? Do the tools represent how the learners will be functioning in "real life"?

Determining the tool and approach…

- Intended outcome
- Nature of the learning task
- Match task with appropriate medium
- Consider profile and needs of learners
- Meta-learning elements required
  (are we trying to teach content or process?)
- Diverse tools/spaces/ecologies

Our technology mediated spaces are becoming adaptive (speech recognition software, or smart agents that "learn" from our activities). The environment in which we function learns from our activity (strengths/weaknesses, test results, interactions). After the environment "knows us" as learners, it adapts, or respond to, our actions. Instead of one-way, same content for all, the system provides personalized content reflective of our true learning needs. Currently, this is prohibitive. Few organizations can afford an implementation of this level. The task of creating an intelligent agent capable of reacting to learner competence and providing personalized content/instruction/interaction, is simply too expensive for anyone but select research institutions and corporations.

If technology is not able to provide affordable adaptability, and educators are constrained by design and time, what is the option? The more completely we exist in multiple domains of knowledge, the more effective the knowledge exchange.

Conversation is the ultimate personalization experience—we ask questions and offer views based on our own conceptions. We personalize our knowledge when we socialize.

As we add social dimensions to our cognition, we can create an adaptive model that learns based on the activities of all members in a space. Consider a class with 30 learners—communicating in transparent ways— exposing their thoughts and ideas for others. When we aggregate their combined voices, we are able to see how they are/are not "getting the content." Their knowledge needs will most certainly not be fully met by the work of the instructor. As voices of learners are aggregated, knowledge gaps will emerge permitting the *gurus* of the space to supplement missing areas. Instead of a canned course on Macbeth, we can provide a learning experience that adapts to learners' needs based on how they interact and learn. The entire ecology of learning is the accurate whole.

THE LEARNER IS THE TEACHER IS THE LEARNER.

Connections provide the greatest value when they generate a certain type of content for the learner. It is not content in general that we want. *We want content that is current, relevant, and contextually appropriate.* Connections are the devices that enable this to occur. Consider an employee who is working on site and needs to access a product manual (current, relevant). The contextually appropriate format (cell phone, laptop, PDA) makes the content more useful. Contrast this with traditional knowledge sharing. A manual (or training classroom) rarely meets the criteria of current/relevant/contextually appropriate. Much of a corporation's knowledge provision to employees occurs in advance of need (which is useful in forming mindsets, but not too effective for skill transfer), and presents content in a static *point-in-time* manner.

Knowledge has to be accessible at the point of need. Container-views of knowledge, artificially demarcated (courses, modules) for communication, are restrictive for this type of flow and easy-access learning.

It is also worth considering what happens when we create connections between content—we create a network or aggregation of different ideas...which adds meaning (pattern recognition) to the individual voices. *Connections change content.* Content is imbued with new meaning when situated in a network (or is it more accurate to say that the network acquires new meaning when new content is added?). Either perspective validates the importance of creating connections over content. When the network is sufficiently large to account for diverse perspectives, it achieves a certain level of meaning that is reflective of the combined force of individual elements.

Our relationship to content has to change when content creation accelerates. We can no longer consume all relevant content items.

The capacity to stay current is more important than any individual content element.

Currency of knowledge is the function of a network, and raising the value of skills of network-making. The network becomes a separate cognitive element—it processes, filters, evaluates, and validates new information. If content has a short lifespan (as new information is acquired), then it would logically imply that our education and training systems should not be about content in particular—they should specifically be about current content.

In a connectivist approach to learning, we create networks of knowledge to assist in replacing outdated content with current content. We off-load many cognitive capabilities onto the network, so that our focus as learners shifts from processing to pattern recognition. When we off-load the processing elements of cognition, we are able to think, reason, and function at a higher level (or navigate more complex knowledge spaces).

We have treated the learner and the content as one entity. We fill the learner with content and release them into the corporate world. As their content runs low, they attend evening/continuing education classes in order to *refill*. This model works fairly well when the half-life of knowledge (how long it takes for knowledge to lose relevance) is long.

When we stop seeing knowledge as an entity that is possessed within a person and start to cast it as a function of elements distributed across a system, we notice a dramatic impact on the education process: the educator becomes a supporter (not the center), the content is not as critical as the connections, learners find value in their aggregated perspectives, learners become content creators, and learning is continuous, exploratory, and sustained (not controlled or filtered by only one agent).

In today's world, knowledge life is short; it survives only a short period of time before it is outdated. Most individuals need to spend an enormous amount of time in continuing education classes to stay current. It is not good for business, and it is not good for an employee's sanity.

We need to separate the learner from the knowledge they hold. It is not really as absurd as it sounds. Consider the tools and processes we currently use for learning. Courses are static, textbooks are written years before actual use, classrooms are available at set times, and so on. The underlying assumption of corporate training and higher education centers on the notion that the world has not really changed.

But it has. Employees cannot stay current by taking a course periodically. Content distribution models (books and courses) cannot keep pace with information and knowledge growth. Problems are becoming so complex that they cannot be contained in the mind of one individual—problems are held in a distributed manner across networks, with each node holding a part of the entire puzzle. Employees require the ability to rapidly form connections with other *specialized* nodes (people or knowledge objects). Rapidly creating connections with others results in a more holistic view of the problem or opportunity, a key requirement for decision making and action in a complex environment.

How do we separate the learner from the knowledge? By focusing not on the content they need to know (content changes constantly and requires continual updating), but on the connections to nodes which continually filter and update content.

This model is not without controversy. Many disparage the work of Wikipedia as informal, unprofessional, and lacking authenticity. While a valid complaint in many situations,[48] it is important to recognize that the function of emerging knowledge tools is to match knowledge's pace and adaptability. To be completely accurate in one instance is to be inaccurate completely when core elements change. *To be adaptive is to be perpetually current.* Weinberger states that some knowledge is simply "good enough," and as an object, it "is social…as flawed as we are."[49]

CONNECTIVISM, as a staged view of how individuals encounter and explore knowledge in a networked/ecological manner, follows the following path (beginning with the basic and moves to the more complex):

Awareness . . . Individuals acquire basic skills
and Receptivity   for handling information abundance,
                   have access t o resources and tools.

Connection. . . . Individuals begin to use tools and
    Forming   and understanding acquired during level one
                   to create and form a personal network. They are
                   active in the learning ecology/space in terms of
                   consuming or acquiring new resources and tools.
                   Selection (filtering) skills are important. Affective/
                   emotive factors play a prominent role in deciding
                   which resources to add to the personal learning
                   network.

Contribution and . . . Individuals are fairly comfortable within
    Involvement   within their self-created network (though
                   experts may continue to guide and direct their
                   access to valuable resources). The learner begins to
                   actively contribute to the network/ecology—
                   essentially, becoming a "visible node." The learner's
                   active contribution and involvement allows other
                   nodes on the network to acknowledge his/her
                   resources, contributions, and ideas—creating
                   reciprocal relationships and shared understandings
                   (or, if social technology is used, collaboratively-
                   created understanding). They should also be
                   capable of choosing the right tool for the right
                   learning task. For example, the learner may opt to
                   take a course, attend a conference, solicit a mentor,

or subscribe to news feeds—all based on what they needs to know, do, or believe. Selecting the right element within the learning ecology is valuable in ensuring the efficiency and effectiveness of the learning process.

Pattern Recognition. . Individuals are network aware and competent. As dynamic participants in the ecology, they have moved from passive content consumption to active contribution. Time in the network has resulted in the learner developing an increased sense of what is happening in the network/ecology as a whole. Having mastered the basics of being a participant, they are now capable to recognize emerging patterns and trends. Experience within the network has resulted in an understanding the nuances of the space (online or physical). The longer an individual spends in the learning space, the more adept she/he will become at recognizing new patterns or *changing winds* of information and knowledge.

Meaning-Making . . . Individuals are capable of understanding *meaning*. What do the emerging patterns mean? What do changes and shifts in trends mean? How should the learner, adjust, adapt, and respond? Meaning-making is the foundation of action and reformation of view points, perspectives, and opinions.

Praxis . . . Individuals are actively involved in tweaking, building, and recreating their own learning network. Metacognition (thinking about thinking) plays a prominent role as they evaluate which elements in the network serve useful purposes and which elements need to be eliminated. The learner is also focused on active reflection of the shape of the ecology itself. The learner may engage in attempts to transform the ecology beyond his/her own network. Praxis, as a cyclical process of reflection, experimentation, and action, allows the learner to critically evaluate the tools, processes, and elements of an ecology or network.

Ultimately, whether online, face-to-face, or blended, learning and knowledge environments need to be democratic and diverse. A critical concept to keep in mind: the network and ecology must both be dynamic and capable of evolving, adapting, and responding to external change. The praxis level ensures that the personal learning network is relevant and current.

Learning is continual. It is not an activity that occurs outside of our daily lives. We have shifted from life stopping when we learn; going to school for two-four years, while not working…to learning in synch with life; constant, ongoing—accretion level as presented in Figure 19.

LEARNING IN SYNCH WITH LIFE

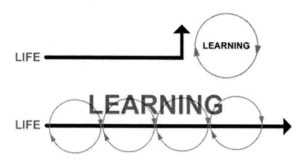

Figure 19. Learning in Synch with Life

Unfortunately, many of our ideas, methods, and theories of learning "impede genuine practice of the attitudes and actions that should constitute lifelong learning."[50]

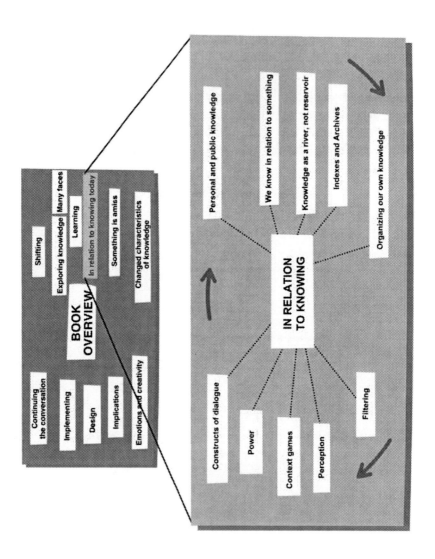

Figure 20. In Relation to Knowing

In Relation
TO KNOWING

Knowledge exists in public and personal spaces. Publicly, knowledge is created and shaped by the combined activity of many. Personally, knowledge has meaning when it is something that we have experienced, encountered, or connected ourselves.

Viewing knowledge as therapy or diagnosis is more holistic than viewing knowledge as a theory or mechanical model. A thing is revealed only when we see it for what it is, not for how we would have it be.

Organizations "know how" to do things. Large-scale complicated projects cannot be known entirely by any single individual. The combined knowledge of many is required:
-- to build machines like air planes, nuclear submarines, or
-- to undergo processes like discovering a new pharmaceutical, or
-- to experience the challenge of exploring complex functionality like stock markets and weather systems.

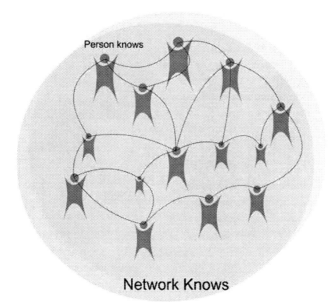

Figure 21. Personal and Public Knowledge

Why do we want Knowledge and what do we want to do with It?

The more we desire knowledge for our intended purposes, the more inclined we are to filter and select based on our goals. The story of knowledge becomes more about us and less about letting knowledge speak for itself.

We know in relation to something. When we encounter a viewpoint, we bring the weight of our recent experiences, our established beliefs, and the emotions of our day to bear. We dialogue and debate based partly on our principles, but mostly in relation to what is occurring around us. Speak to me today, and I may have strong opinions about the role of software in democracy. Speak to me tomorrow, and I may advocate for open-source software to serve the collective. Speak to me next week, and I may advocate for centralized approaches to managing foundation-level learning.

I speak based on where I am situated within my personal learning network…and the context in which I exist. It depends on what I am reacting to.

To know is to be in a particular state of relation (or to share a pattern of meaning)—organized in a certain way that now enables greater end-user involvement. The organization and connection of knowledge does not occur exclusively in the activities of others—we can create/form our own organization schemes.

> To "know" something is to be organized in a certain way, to exhibit patterns of connectivity.
>
> *Stephen Downes*[51]

Knowledge itself is strongly relational—it connects to other knowledge. Researchers suggest our brains are actually pained by new information—a disruption that taxes our thinking (it is easier to function from long-term memory than to actively make sense and function in our conscious short-term memory (or working area) of our brain)[52]. The more connective a knowledge stream, the more valuable. The more we know of how a society functions…or how computers work, the more holistic our understanding…and as a result, the more complete. It is (obviously) possible to know more if we already possess a large knowledge base.

Generally, a psychologist can learn the nuances of a new theory of motivation much more rapidly than a farmer. What is new connects with what is known and is placed within a concept network in the appropriate place.

To know today means to be connected. Knowledge moves too fast for learning to be only a product. We used to acquire knowledge by bringing it close to ourselves. We were said to possess it—to have it exist in our heads. We can no longer seek to possess all needed knowledge personally. We must store it in our friends or within technology.

> *Experience has long been considered the best teacher of knowledge. Since we cannot experience everything, other people's experiences, and hence other people, become the surrogate for knowledge. 'I store my knowledge in my friends' is an axiom for collecting knowledge through collecting people.*
>
> *Karen Stephenson[53]*

The elements that create understanding are scattered across many structures and spaces. We "know" when we seek and pull elements together—when we create a meaning-laden view of an entity.

The new value point for knowledge is the capacity for awareness, connection, and recombination/re-creation.

Elements have inherent characteristics. Ideas, theories, and knowledge, like physical objects, possess traits that define what they are.

Entities with similar traits possess the possibility of entering an exchange of synchronization[54]. This is a strong argument for some level of objectivity in certain types of knowledge. If similar characteristics are required for synchronization—like fireflies lighting in unison—it provides an impression that nature sees as we see. It is not only our experience of an entity that *makes* it, but it is the inherent characteristics it possesses.

Things synch based on inherent characteristics. A network reflects on itself to create itself. It creates its own "what is."

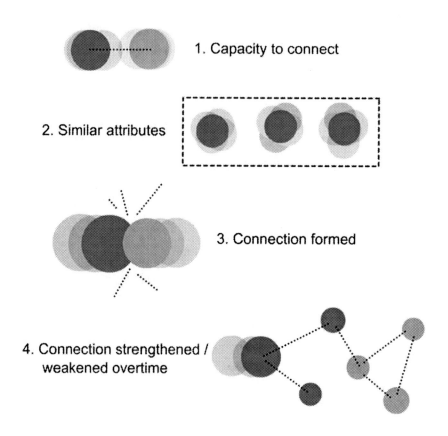

Figure 22. Oscillators Synch Based on Capacity/Similarity

We attempt to synch, but largely our dialogue is in reaction to, or in support of, what is before us. The metrics of logic are similarly influenced by context, space, and elements present. If what is before us is too unlike what is within us, we are not capable of forming a connection.

The capacity for connection forming, becoming aware (of others and knowledge), and sustaining exchanges, lies at the heart of knowledge exchange today. Our design of methods, organizations, and systems benefit most by allowing greatest opportunity for connectivity. The capacity to connect produces the capacity to adapt.

We have in the past seen knowledge as an object and learning as a product. But knowledge is really more of a stream...and learning more of a process. *A product is a stopped process*—consider a book, building a car, a course, a training program, a marketing campaign.

The end of process is the product. Our internet-era knowledge is no longer suitable as a product—we can continue to revise, connect, and alter indefinitely.

Knowledge as a river, not reservoir

Process, not product

Figure 23. Knowledge as a River, not Reservoir

Certain types of knowledge may still pool (much like types of knowledge are hardened through expert validation and public consensus). With ongoing development of technology, cross-industry collaboration, global connectedness and competitiveness, more and more knowledge moves with river-like properties.

> Any piece of knowledge I acquire today has a value at this moment exactly proportioned to my skill to deal with it.
> Mark Van Doren[55]

Our knowledge spaces consist of libraries (indexes) and encyclopedias (archives), with varying dimensions of disseminating tools (journals, books, conferences). We are currently carrying the inefficiencies of these spaces into the digital realm. As a result, we are still trying to create certainty with our knowledge. We are trying to store knowledge for future retrieval (Google indexes, Wikipedia archives). We do not yet have the tool that permits "stepping into the stream."

Library catalogues and encyclopedias attempt to put knowledge into a reservoir—to categorize and structure it in a manner that *makes sense*. This is rooted in traditional conceptions of knowing: ontology and epistemology.

The issue is deeper.

Could knowing be far more a function of context than constructs of evaluation created in advance of use? A catalogue system determines the shape of a field. When new information is added, it is placed into a previously created file/folder/categorization. When knowledge becomes fluid, categories are less useful. Individuals create a network of the knowledge space during the process of knowledge emerging, not in advance. This is a significant distinction—one that will have substantial impact on both corporations and higher education.

Indexes create an unconnected knowledge space that requires integration and effort on our part, in order to answer questions and tackle problems. The cognitive load is higher in this unstructured knowledge space, but the metrics of "what can be known" are still based on traditional epistemology. Once we have acquired knowledge from indexes, we put them into some manner of categorization that is reflective of what happens in Britannica/Wikipedia.

We are too impatient with knowledge. We categorize it by imposing our models of organization.

Instead of experts and others defining what knowledge is and how it is to be organized, we can organize and create it in a manner that suits our needs (at that point in time).

If we perceive knowledge to be a stream (the daily knowledge that flows across our desks, computers, conversations, books), then at certain points, we need the ability to access or RE-FIND information/knowledge when it is needed.

WHICH TOOLS enable us to make use of the incredibly diverse nature of knowledge and application?

Tools today serve a purpose that is largely based on the "old" model of library catalogue and encyclopedia. As categorization (and finding) models, they serve a purpose when we have a one-dimensional relationship to knowledge (namely that we understand we need it and, in the process, seek to acquire it). What happens when software/technology does this for us? What happens when the knowledge we require is presented to us without having to consciously seek it (artificial intelligence)?

We manage the daily flow of knowledge in and out of our lives through a sloppy mix of tools and processes, evidenced by the growth of blogs, wikis, social bookmarking, and tags. It works for a percentage of the population, but the tools themselves need to be mainstreamed through ease of use and integration.

Different tools serve different functionality—an index is great for non-connected knowledge about which we can form an opinion. The organized knowledge of an archive is great when we want to quickly *consume* someone else's opinion.

The ability to organize knowledge as we want it is a defining characteristic of our era. In the past, knowledge has been defined for us through editors, teachers, and experts. Now we do the organization ourselves. Traditionally (and Wikipedia still duplicates the physical model of an encyclopedia) knowledge was crafted/combined/filtered. With the predicted rapid influx of new knowledge (the era which we are just entering), we need a different model. The model needs to be aligned with knowledge itself.

Knowledge is still seen as something we hold/possess based on its merits or application. This model will change quickly. Knowledge will be less of a product, and more of a process—an integrated means of updating established knowledge stores, so that when something changes, it is reflected in the repository (index/archive). The initial context of use that required an individual to select the knowledge in the first place will be reflected in how they receive updated knowledge. This concept will be explored in greater detail later in the form of *knowledge reflexivity.*

Technology will be increasingly depended upon to mediate the bulk of our current knowledge seeking behavior. We spend much of our time seeking and trying to locate what we need—findability is still a primary knowledge behavior. Once knowledge is more tightly integrated in contexts of use, we can shift more attention to the act of application. We need to move beyond finding and evaluating relevance, to use and application.

Is serendipity lost?

When we filter knowledge ourselves, we risk losing the serendipity of random encounters. The value of personal control may reduce diverse experiences beyond our intention. So much of what comprises new knowledge today is actually transvergence—transferred from another domain, but relevant and capable of filling in missing gaps. Transvergence is facilitated by serendipitous collisions with knowledge outside of our conscious interests. We need those random moments of being exposed to new thoughts and experiences.

Serendipity requires people of diverse interests, interacting in unstructured spaces. Structured systems perpetuate (and favor) structure. Greater levels of diversity require individuals to communicate, share, and be transparent with each other. The combined voices involved in communication results in an open space where the voices of many flesh out and define an issue, concern, or topic. The "wisdom of crowds" only works when each member of the collective brings a unique perspective to the space[56]. If we do not permit individuality, we end up closing doors of creativity. Tools of individuality serve a greater good to society than tools of purely collective traits. Collectivity requires individual voices—combined—not overwritten. Unique individuals, engaged in dialogue, lay the foundation for serendipitous encounters and the ability for ideas to germinate as they come in contact with other ideas.

Knowing is a *transitory* state in that what is known changes during the internal cycle of knowing (caterpillar to butterfly) and through development and use.

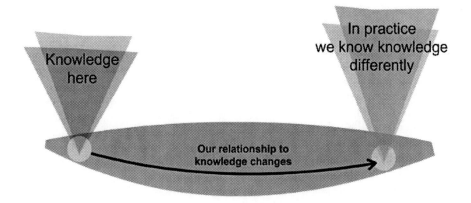

Figure 24. Knowledge Changes in Practice

Consider an individual who knows of Paris, France. She might be acquainted with alternate terms—city of lights, or famous landmarks and tourist attractions—Eiffel Tower. In practice, to visit France is a very different type of knowledge. To dine at L'Absinthe or to view Paris from the Eiffel Tower (sights, sounds, smells) produces a deeper, more contextualized form of knowledge.

We experience pieces—we cannot perceive the whole…our thoughts exist in space and time (see Figure 12). To gain one perspective is to leave another. When we experience knowledge in application, we leave theoretical understanding of knowledge.

We connect more than we construct.

Connections create structures. Structures do not create (though they may facilitate) connections. Our approaches today reflect this error in thinking. We have tried to do the wrong thing first with knowledge. We determine that we will have a certification before we determine what it is that we want to certify. We need to enable the growth of connections and observe the structures that emerge

Language is structural (you are a pragmatic, you are an existentialist). We put things into boxes afforded by our language and symbols. Language assigns absolutes where shades exist.

Connections create structure, but only after elements have been considered (the elements contribute to the formation of the structure). We require a model that does the reverse—namely forms structures based on interaction of elements and patterns. Emergence, not predefinition, reflects today's needs.

Our pre-conceived structures of interpreting knowledge sometimes interfere with new knowledge.

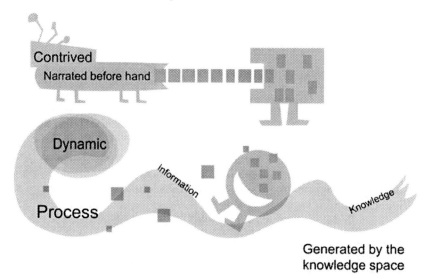

Figure 25. Filtering in Advance. . . or . . . Through the Process

We come to know in many ways:

- ◉ through senses, observation, and experience
- ◉ through thinking and logic
- ◉ through intuition ("gut feel")
- ◉ through revelation (the "Aha" moment of learning or claims held by many religious people)
- ◉ through authority (validated, trusted)
- ◉ through connections (our personal learning network)

Understanding is aided by the metaphors of learning that exist in a particular culture or age. We evaluate through a framework (apply and contrast with what is known). These frameworks sometimes incorrectly filter out needed knowledge. The framework of knowledge filtering in traditional industries (like music, newspaper, and movies) largely excluded emerging core changes, resulting in industries moving in opposite directions from customers. Declines in these industries are largely due to offering a product or service mismatched to the needs and interests of a changing customer base.[57] To perceive in relation to actual societal trends requires a malleable framework, capable of seeing what exists, instead of deselecting elements not in line with our thinking.

Our experience and learning influence how we see new situations and problems. We are less skilled at analyzing knowledge through a network. Hierarchies and linearity are more familiar. We do not know how to flow in a network

We are a bricolage of cognition, emotion, intuition, information consumption, doubt, and belief.

The adoption of a particular belief and mindset will hold within it certain accompanying views and logical developments which are less a function of reasoning and logic and more a function of the space we have decided to enter (see Figure 26). The ideas contain in themselves a germinating process.

The true point of knowing occurs at the stage of creating or adopting an ideology or world view. Once adopted, this view serves as a filter and cognitive off-load tool. If our ideology is strongly empirical, we primarily function within this conceptual domain (though we will hold contradictory view points at times—due to context-games that influence what we think and say at various times). The ideology strongly influences the conclusion. The outcome is not only set in our daily activities, but in the process of selecting a world view.

Sensitivity of initial conditions—reasoning is not so much where we end up in a corridor, but the door through which we enter. Once we know the door, we can generally understand where we will end up.

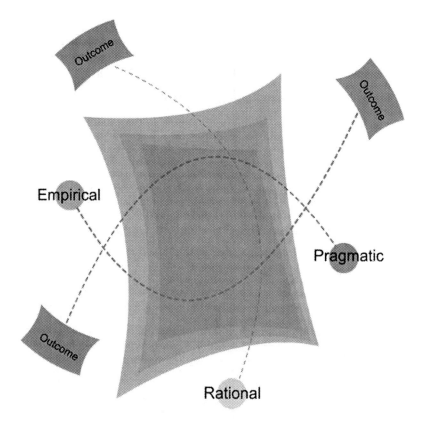

Perception, a neural pathway

Figure 26. Perception and Pathways of Thought

WE SEE TODAY'S PROBLEMS
THROUGH YESTERDAY'S SOLUTIONS.[58]

CONTEXT
GAMES

A conversation is an object. It is formed and frameworked as negotiated by parties.

Attempts to define who we are and why we do what we do, err in the assumption that there is an answer that exists by itself.

We are able to create a framework for understanding more rapidly than at any other time in history. Conversation spaces are readily available. Breakdown and teardown happens in seconds.

...we are not about logic

we are not only about our drives and desires...

We are about Context Games.

Our desires and logic are shaped in an orchestra of context: acting and reacting, negotiating and dialoguing.

To define context is to frame the solution.

Context is not as simple as being in a different space...context includes elements like our emotions, recent experiences, beliefs, and the surrounding environment—each element possesses attributes, that when considered in a certain light, informs what is possible in the discussion. The object is tied to the nature of the discussion (framework [or network] of thought). The context-game is the formulation and negotiation of what will be permissible, valued, and the standards to which we will appeal in situations of dispute. The context-game of implementing a new corporate strategy involves individuals, politics, permissible ways of seeing and perceiving, recent events, corporate history, and a multitude of other factors.

Context games are the attempt to clarify and highlight factors that impact our comprehension of a particular situation.

Consider two individuals engaging in a discussion of liberal and conservative politics. The real discussion is not about a particular political issue (for example, the degree to which the government should be involved in social programs). Instead, the real discussion centers on each party attempting to project their deeper views (based on the "pathway" model provided in Figure 26)—namely that by adopting a view, we often walk to its logical outcome.) We do not engage situations neutrally. We engage them based on the manner in which we have crafted our logic or how we have entered the corridors of logic. We do not evaluate a thing only for "what it is." We evaluate it for how it relates to our defined views and ideologies.

Context games include:

1. What we bring: Our existing viewpoints/ideologies
2. What impacts: The factors that exist and impact the discussion/ knowledge (recent events, news items, networks nodes from which we perceive)
3. What exists: The nature of the topic—it melds with the context and causes ripples of change within the context itself.
4. Space of occurrence: The environment/culture/zeitgeist in which the dialogue/debate occurs
5. Who is involved: Parties with whom we are familiar shape the context; we fill in missing elements based on previous encounters
6. What we possess: Oratory or charismatic traits of the participant
7. What we feel: Emotions
8. What we communicate: The attempt to convey to others the validity of each perspective
9. How we negotiate: How we determine measures of validity and acceptable context (requires give and take)
10. What is the domain, type, state, and level of knowledge?
11. How we debate: The points of logic, emotion, inclusion/exclusion
12. Context breakdown (and archiving for future similar experiences)

In a sense, the key area seen as the surface notion of the debate (in our previous example of government involvement in social programs) is not really an issue. It is an opening through which we can express our larger views.

With regard to knowledge and learning, context influences our capacity to convey our thoughts. If knowledge has been hardened into ideologies, or if new knowledge is seen through ideologies crafted in advance, the outcome of the discussion is essentially set. Debate is largely an attempt to project world views.

Of what value is the act of debate? Debate provides an additional dimension to context that enables individuals to see entities beyond their own worldviews. We categorize and box individuals. This presupposes how they think and act. By understanding context games, we are better able to suspend hard proclamations in advance of understanding the particular concept being expressed by others. If both parties acknowledge context creation activities, the capacity to agree on a particular framework of debate and inclusion of perspectives that may challenge our established ideologies, may be increased. If our debate is less about projecting our world views, and more about exploring what is actually being said, we open our minds to reception of knowledge that is filtered by our opinions.

We value what is different more than what is known…it pulls on logic toward non-logic directions.

Existing mental models are not loose enough to allow for new structure to emerge. Mental models (like schema) assume that we are logical and structured in our exposure to knowledge. We are not always logical.

We are contextually holistic. We act consistent with how we have framed and determined our world. We filter out information we feel is not important. Our behavior is consistent with our context, though we may at times violate our actions of the past.

We do not exclusively subsume, accommodate, or assimilate. We place new knowledge in relation to other knowledge. If similarities exist or revelations occur, the element is connected to our neural structure. *We connect more than we construct.*

What about power?

Is it troubling that knowledge is changing? For some. Who? Those who currently serve as providers of, or gatekeepers to, knowledge.

What about traditional power structures? Is knowledge power? Does the free access to knowledge we currently possess equal a greater shift in power to the consumer? What about the continuing wealth disparity? If it is true that power has shifted to the consumer, where is it evident in our society? Do we have real power—the power to change society, to remake the world? Or is our power as end users restricted to remaking media and uploading images, files, and embarrassing karaoke videos?

If power is shifting to consumers, why are corporations continuing to expand their influence? Is it wishful thinking on our part? Or are the social masses able to balance corporations and governments?[59]

Or is it simply hype? Is technology changing politics? Is it forcing deep changes in our society? Or is our tinkering at the surface, while the hidden hands of power continues to move and shape society? Is our power but one of perception and not deep influence?

Power, like knowledge, is moving from deep reservoirs and is flooding the landscape.

The power to speak exists for everyone. The power to be heard still pools.

Who are the new oppressed?

The oppressed in the digital divide:

1. Those without access to tools of global conversation.
2. Those without skills to contribute to global conversations.

What we decide today creates ripples that will change the landscape or how we decide tomorrow. The aggregate of the many forms the new power base.

Every industry will be impacted as power floods into the lives of individuals: marketing, business, school, publishing, recording/movie industries, churches, and religious bodies.

Is knowing really about thought constructs? Internal representations? Or do the thoughts themselves morph too rapidly to be perceived as a construct? Is it more like patterns held by the aggregate of our neurons—where no one area of our brain holds a *representation?* Perhaps the real concept that we currently call representation is actually the rapid bringing together of dispersed information through neural activity. The representation itself does not exist in its entirety, only in pieces. Connecting, or binding, creates the whole.

In order to bring the pieces together, we rely on patterning. Patterning is the process of recognizing the nature and organization of various types of information and knowledge. The shapes created by these structures will determine how readily new connections can be made.

> *Organizations are not systems but the ongoing patterning of interactions between people. Patterns of human interaction produce further patterns of interaction, not some thing outside of the interaction. We call this perspective complex responsive processes of relating.*
>
> Ralph Stacey[60]

The words we use influence our ability to think, reflect, and react. Language creates structure, though not a framework—a framework is too rigid—boundaries formed through the creation of networks of ideas (note, the boundaries emerge as a result of the network, but once established they shape future network formation).

Opposition to an idea is often less of a commentary on the idea itself and more of a reflection of where the objector is positioned (space and time) in relation to the idea.

We adjust our logic to serve our conclusions. Only a few times in our lives do we build foundations (for example: evolution, creationism). The rest of our time is spent building on these foundations.

> *Reason itself is a matter of faith. It is an act of faith to assert that our thoughts have any relation to reality at all.*
>
> G.K. Chesterton[61]

Our challenge of thinking is the creation and breakdown of structures for dialogue. The content that we debate is of less significance, because how it is processed is a function of the construct itself. We must battle against constructs that are created too early, and as a result, damage our capacity for ongoing learning and functioning.

Knowledge possesses different states. Knowledge that has hardened is typically not open for debate (we rarely enter conversations prepared to alter our core beliefs). We are prepared to create constructs to debate knowledge that is malleable. Where we have created a firm perspective, we are more apt to desire to communicate, rather than dialogue.

Strong opinions, weakly held.

Bob Sutton[62]

Changes and Implications

MOVING
TOWARD
APPLICATION

Figure 27. Change in Environment

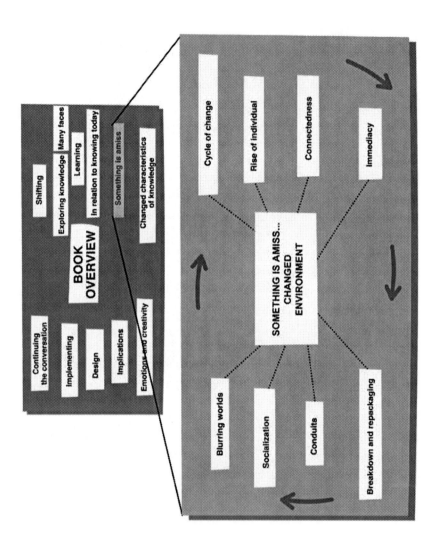

SOMETHING IS AMISS...

Changed environments of knowledge

Change is happening on two levels:

1. ....the context in which knowledge occurs, and
2. ....the flow and characteristics of knowledge itself.

The changing nature and context of knowledge influences everything: scholarship, teaching, research, corporate structure, leadership, marketing. The industrial age reconfigured society. Cottage industries gave way to corporations. Business structure emerged as hierarchy (to better facilitate the movement and organization of physical goods).

We are at a similar place. Our society is being restructured to align with knowledge. The barriers, inhibitors, obstacles, and unnecessary structures are giving away to models which permit effective knowledge creation, dissemination, communication, personalization, and flow.

As Richard Restak states,

> Yesterday's predictions have become today's reality. And in the course of that makeover, we have become more frenetic, more distracted, more fragmented—in a word, more hyperactive.[63]

Cycle of Change

Change pressures arise from different sectors of a system. At times it is mandated from the top of a hierarchy, other times it forms from participants at a grass-roots level. Some changes are absorbed by the organization without significant impact on, or alterations of, existing methods. In other cases, change takes root. It causes the formation of new methods (how things are done and what is possible) within the organization (see Figure 28).

Initially these methods will be informal as those aspects of the organization nearest to the change begin to adapt. Over time, the methods significantly impact the organization, resulting in the creation of new structures and new spaces (an alignment to the nature of change).

These structures and spaces then create new affordances enabling the organization to change and adapt. The new affordances create a new cycle of change pressures.

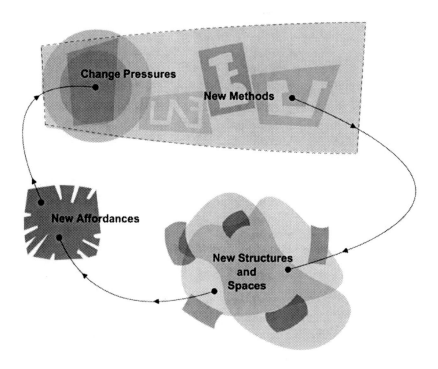

Figure 28. Change Cycle

The fault of many schools, universities, and companies is the unwillingness to listen to the voices of those closest to change pressures and emerging methods.

> *Distributed control means that the outcomes of a complex adaptive system emerge from a process of self-organization rather than being designed and controlled externally or by a centralized body.*
>
> *Zimmerman, Lindberg, & Plsek[64]*

> When the rate of change outside exceeds
> the rate of change inside,
> the end is in sight.
>
> Jack Welch[65]

Change is shaping a new reality under the fabric of our daily lives. Seven broad societal trends are changing the environment in which knowledge exists:

1. The rise of the individual
2. Increased connectedness
3. Immediacy and now
4. Breakdown and repackaging
5. Prominence of the conduit
6. Socialization
7. Blurring worlds of physical and virtual

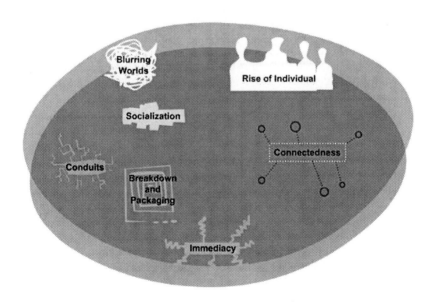

Figure 29. Changes in Environment of Knowledge

The Rise of the Individual

Individuals have more control, more capacity to create and to connect than in any era in history.

Relationships are defined by convenience and interest not geography. We can work wherever and whenever. Time and space no longer limit global conversations.

People are able to connect, share, and create. We are co-creators, not knowledge consumers. Content generation is in the hands of the many. Co-creation is an expression of self...a sense of identity...ownership. We own who we are by the contributions we make.

We are no longer willing to have others think for us. We want to read what concerns us. Listen to what we want. We want only the pieces that interest us, and we want to repackage it so that it makes sense to us.

Repackaging is the personalization of the knowledge created by others.

IDENTITY—we know and can be known. We scatter our lives and thoughts across the web. Each question in a forum, each thought in a blog, each podcast, each comment to an article—these distributed pieces are splashed across the internet. They form who we are, how we think (at a certain time), and the things we believe. We are known by what we have done and said, and what others have said about us. We are laid bare.

Surprisingly, the rise of the individual creates the capacity for collaboration, socialization, and "doing things together." We expect to co-create and experience the two-way flow models of knowledge sharing and dissemination. Our identities are exposed, revealed for anyone to explore.

Weinberger recognized individuals are able to "complexify the simple."[66] Instead of seeing knowledge from only one perspective (the filter), we, as individuals, can contribute our opinions and views to extend the depth (diversity) of our understanding. Knowledge can now be expressed through the aggregate of the individuals—a deafening crescendo of contrasting and complementing opinions and views.

CONNECTEDNESS–the World has Become Whole

Connections raise the potential for adaptation. The power of the human brain is derived from the capacity of each neuron to form many connections. Entities capable of connection-forming are capable of adapting. The greater the number of connections possible, the more adaptive the organization.

We are being remade by our connectivity. As everything becomes connected, everything becomes transparent. Technology illuminates what was not discernable to the human eye.

We can connect where-ever (space breakdown). We can connect when-ever (time breakdown).

Connectedness allows individuals to create and distribute their own materials and identity. Instead of seeing a whole, we see the many pieces that comprise the whole, and as individuals, we can create the whole that suits our needs and interests.

Everything integrates with everything. Biologists use the language and concepts of physicists. Psychologists use the language of neurologists. Discoveries in one domain ripple across the network of human knowledge. Doors pried open in one discipline reveal corridors sought by others.

When knowledge stops existing in physical spaces, we can duplicate (or connect) entities in multiple spaces. Knowledge, when digital (not in physical entities like paper-based journals and books), can be combined (or remixed) readily with new knowledge. Bringing together ideas from two different books requires effort to bring the entities together (buy both books or go to the library). With digital knowledge, we can link (as David Weinberger famously wrote: "hyperlinks subvert hierarchies"[67]) and bring two ideas together with ease.

IMMEDIACY

Everything is now. Knowledge flows in real time. Global conversations are no longer restricted by physical space. The world has become immediate. New information changes markets in minutes. New programs are written in hours, building on the openness and work of others. Leaders must know what happened five minutes ago, not only what happened yesterday. Our filters of information and knowledge assume delays and stopping points, so we can assess implications.

The flow does not stop today. We must develop real-time processing tools, so we can make sense of the unabated flow. We must develop skills to select what is important, store what is needed for the future, and ensure our decisions are based on knowledge that is current. Interpretation and decision-making need to happen in the same speed and spirit as the knowledge flow.

REFLECTION (the act of thought on our actions, motivations, experiences, and world events) is becoming a lost art. Deriving meaning no longer happens at a *pause point*. Meaning is derived in real time.

The beauty of life always resides below the surface of busyness. How can we appreciate the quietness? Has our generation moved beyond contemplation and silence to distraction and motion? How is our humanness changed?

Does immediacy cause us to be driven not by principles, but by existing context? While context is significant in every knowledge interaction, is it a good leader? What are our guides today? Have higher ideals yielded to the now?

Our lives are being consumed by "now."

Breakdown and Repackaging

It is all in pieces. Knowledge is unmoored. The selection, flow, and discussion of knowledge have all moved from controlled spaces (at the point of creation or filtering) to the domain of the consumer. We take small pieces. We mix them. We create personal understandings.

Shared understandings happen only when we absorb similar patterns as others…or when we create shared patterns. Today, we receive our news, our entertainment, our learning, from distributed means. Two people in the same household stitch together different understandings based on the pieces each used.

We have centering spaces where we share understandings—communities, but we all belong to different communities. We all absorb different information. We all see different knowledge quilts.

How can we relate?

In order to make sense, we extract patterns. While the world of knowledge has gone to pieces, knowledge at point-of-use requires wholeness. We still require centralization. The clearer the aim, the more critical the central model is.

Media develops conversations. Conversations develop reality.

THE CONDUIT IS KING

Content. Context. Conduit: These shape the meaning of knowledge.

    CONTENT . . . begins the knowledge cycle.

    CONTEXT . . . makes it meaningful

    CONDUIT . . . makes it relevant, current, and available.

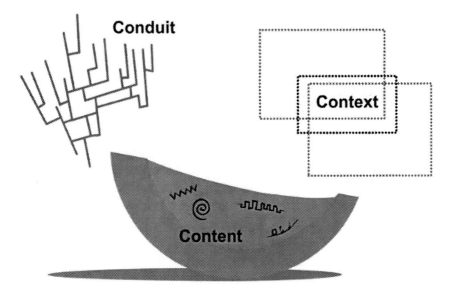

Figure 30. Content/Context/Conduit

Our perception of content is too prominent in the knowledge process. When we talk knowledge and learning, we think of content—books, articles, audio files, and video clips.

But knowledge today changes that. Connections are possible with anyone, almost anytime. Emerging collaborative technologies are continuing to extend our potential to connect to content and people, but in the process, it also alters content. Content development pace increases.

WHAT IS THE IMPACT?

Due to rapid changes, we need to continually reference original content. But this is a big challenge. Our tools and approaches are not very friendly toward quickly changing content.

Learning and knowledge networks are correcting the existing deficiency of connections, in relation to content. In part, connections need to take a prominent role, because connections permit the formation of new content (content is sub-servant to connections).

Learning is *not* content consumption. Learning happens during some process of interaction and reflection.   Content, then, can be a lead into learning...or it can be a by-product of the learning process.

We MUST blend content with context and conduits.

Connections, on the other hand, are a more direct lead into learning, simply because connections are more vibrant than content. Connections are more social and action-oriented than content.

Transfer this thinking to corporate environments: What is more important? What is currently known (existing content/knowledge)? Our capacity to continue to know more (connections)?

Connection-forming tools will always create content, but their value lies in our ability to reflect on, dialogue about, and internalize content in order to learn. Content is knowledge frozen at a certain time (a magazine article), whereas a connection is a pipeline to continue to flow new knowledge.

SOCIALIZATION

Socialization is an affordance of connectedness.

We are now able to socialize our activities to an unprecedented level. Technology is opening doors to conversation. Every nuance, every characteristic, can be dissected and represented in multiple ways and perspectives. The notion of what is known is confused with limitless viewpoints. Certainty is clouded by multiplicity.

We socialize with others of like interest from around the world. Everyone, no matter how out of place physically, has a mirrored companion digitally. These mirror identities and interests, however, are not without fault. We can build closed spaces where we dialogue with others who share our viewpoints...and we are no longer forced to think critically as we casually encounter contrasting views (while watching a television newscast or reading a journal article). We simply echo our beliefs to each other.[68]

Everyone builds, produces, creates, talks. Have we merged talking with listening? When we create on the work of others, is listening the act of speaking how we interpret their perspective? In an age where everyone has a voice to broadcast, our need to listen and understand becomes more prominent.

The ability to connect with those of like-minds and beliefs compresses diversity. We must now intentionally seek views that are unlike ours. We can now exist in our own spaces and hear only those things with which we agree.

Polarization is intensified.

BLURRING WORLDS

Physical and virtual realities are blurring. Our space of existence has been defined by duality: PHYSICAL and DIGITAL (virtual). Those distinctions are rapidly changing. We buy with digital money. We build digital spaces. We exist in online worlds.

We can collaborate, run businesses, find romance, share ideas, create new software, and shape a new world—all with people we have never seen. We are developing our collective ability to function under a new skill set.

When we meet face-to-face, we are skilled at interpreting and analyzing meaning; a furrowed brow... a smirk... a raised eyebrow. We know how to function in the physical. We are learning how to function in the virtual. Tone of voice blended with the message. First text, then audio, now video. We can come to know each other without touching.

We blend our virtual interactions with face-to-face. Our water cooler conversations driven by last night's newscast, the comic strip in the morning paper, are replaced with discussions of video logs, or content presented online (personalizing the internet with our views).

The creator, the consumer have become one.

The membrane between real and virtual is thinning.

We are starting to exist simultaneously in each.[69]

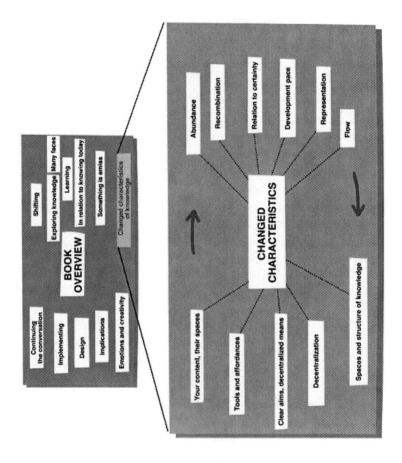

Figure 31. Knowledge Change

Changed Characteristics &
FLOW OF KNOWLEDGE

The climate in which knowledge occurs has changed, but so have the characteristics and flow of knowledge.

Changes in the context of knowledge run parallel to change in knowledge characteristics. The physiological and chemical process of recalling, storing, deriving meaning are likely the same as they were in decades past, with some evidence emerging that technology is changing the manner in which we think. Earl Miller, Massachusetts Institute of Technology, states: "We physically rewire our brain so we process our environment."[71] Other researchers share the view of brain rewiring through technology use: "This clearly implies a direct relationship between our brain's organization and operation and what we can learn about the world and about ourselves as part of that world."[72]

While we may only be at the beginning stages of chemical changes or rewiring of our minds (and research is still continuing to emerge), the characteristics of knowledge are changing noticeably.

8 broad factors define the characteristics of knowledge today:

1. Abundance
2. Capacity for recombination
3. Certainty…for now
4. Pace of development
5. Representation through media
6. Flow
7. Spaces and structures of knowledge organization and dissemination
8. Decentralization

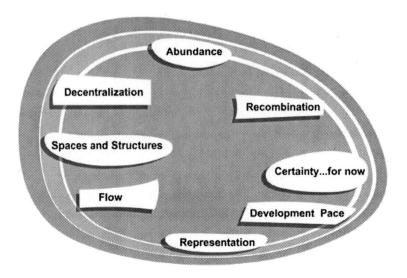

Figure 32. Changes in Knowledge

ABUNDANCE

In one generation we have moved from knowledge as value points, to our ability to manage the abundance as the value point.

It has exploded.[73] We have always had access to more knowledge than we were able to handle. It has intensified in our generation. Increased global connectedness, socialization, and other factors discussed previously, are accelerating change and knowledge growth. We can not keep up. Our ability to **pay attention** is overwhelmed.

> *Why is our attention so valuable? Because it is so scarce or, more accurately, because its relative scarcity has been rapidly increasing. Attention is a constant resource for each of us— we only have 24 hours in the day. It is up to us how we use those 24 hours. What's changed is that we have more and more options competing for our attention. We face increasing abundance both in the production and distribution of goods and information about those goods.*
>
> *John Hagel[74]*

Knowledge depreciates rapidly when new knowledge is constantly being created. The life-span of knowledge is shrinking. An expectancy of relevance and currency of knowledge for a cycle of years and decades, has now been reduced to months and years for many disciplines. Fifty years ago, education prepared an individual for a life-long career in a particular field. Formal education created the person, the opportunity. Now, lifelong learning creates the opportunity.

Dealing with knowledge abundance requires new skills. *Hitting a stationary target requires different skills of a marksman than hitting a target in motion.* Our work requires tracking targets in motion. We assume that knowledge is a stationary target—namely a status that we achieve or a product that we acquire.

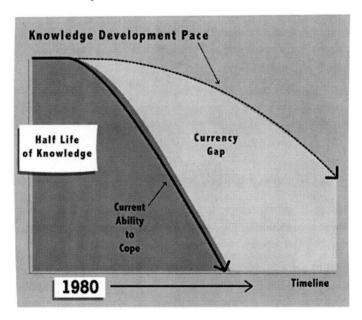

Figure 33. Half Life of Knowledge

The half-life of knowledge is the time required for half of the knowledge in a field to be rendered obsolete due to new developments, research, innovations, or changed climate.[75] Different types of knowledge will have a different half-life (physics and mathematical formulas have a longer life than discoveries within nanotechnology).[76]

RECOMBINATION

The ability to connect, recombine, and recreate are hallmarks of knowledge today. Small pieces, which stand on their own, can be recreated in different media, contexts, and used to create more personalized, complex structures. The material used to build a car must be put together in a precise manner in order for the vehicle to function. Knowledge can be woven, connected, and recombined in limitless ways…creating the possibility of personalized networks of knowledge.

BUILDING BLOCKS BECOME BUILDING BLOCKS BECOME BUILDING BLOCKS.

Knowledge has hooks. It can be organized and arranged in a myriad of ways. Recombination occurs in the spaces of debate and dialogue. An individual with a computer and internet connection can access MIT's OpenCourseWare[77] resources—learning, building, creating, blending, and extending. Knowledge can be connected (combined, recreated) as is desired by the individual.

No longer is convergence the cry of knowledge. TRANSVERGENCE (the transfer and application of knowledge from one field to another) is the new reality. The world is connected. We are becoming aware of activities outside of our own spaces.

RELATION TO CERTAINTY

Knowledge is not directly related to certainty. We think that "to know" means to abolish doubt. But knowledge is often more about knowing that we do not know…where *not knowing is held in context.*

Certain things we can know with certainty, but only for now. The pressures of change form quickly from non-traditional corners. Developing countries, the masses, the oppressed—all can be partakers in shaping the direction the wind of knowledge blows.

Our quest for certainty (is that not why we seek knowledge?) is challenged today. When we discover something new, someone else will build on and extend it (transvergence), or new research will prove it untrue. Or foundational conditions will change, requiring the discovery to be updated.

Continual suspended certainty is today's reality. States of "not knowing" are healthy.

Does all knowledge change? Is nothing certain?

DEVELOPMENT PACE

Books take years to publish. Conferences take months to plan. Magazines take weeks to write. TV newscasts take hours to produce. End user created media takes minutes to produce and circulate.

The filter of time, to take the edge off of reactionism, is torn away. Events are deciphered in real time. The ferocity of responses, views, and dissemination walks a path of passion, not cold reason.

What is a leader to do? How do we stay current, but sane, when the buffers on emotion are loosed?

> To function in the development pace of society today,
> we are required to rethink our skills and processes.

Is it possible to consume and assimilate the deluge of knowledge in our fields? Is it possible to stay informed of other fields that impact our own? How can we shift our capacity (individual, collective, organizational, and societal), to embrace a world in flux? How can we match our habits of functioning to the pace of knowledge?

The pipe is more important than the content within. Our ability to learn what we need for tomorrow is more important than what we know today. When knowledge is needed, but not known, the ability to plug into sources to meet the requirements becomes vital. As knowledge continues to grow and evolve, access to what is needed is more important than what the learner currently possesses.

REPRESENTATION

> "*Any understanding of social and cultural change is impossible without a knowledge of the way media works as environments.*"

Marshall McLuhan[78]

Ours is a world shaped by diversity—text, video, audio, games, and simulations represent ideas, concepts, and emotions. The power of text fails to cast its shadow as broadly as previously. The creators of knowledge do well to think beyond text.

The passivity of text is disturbed by media.

Images, video, and audio now communicate the breadth of our experience with emotion and life. A picture released by an observer in a disaster zone (war, hurricane, earthquake) is worth many times more than the commentary of an expert. An image sears the brain "lending immediacy to images of disaster."[79]

Knowledge is amplified in the multiplicity of representation choices. The multiplicity inherent in knowledge is now expressed by many individuals…in different ways. Organizational views of knowledge must align with our new complexity. Is an essay as effective as a podcast? Is a memo as effective as a video log? Context, resources, and needs determine the suitable approach.

Varied media representations are penetrating our daily lives. We are the constantly watched. Camera phones, online social spaces, digital thoughts—our lives are archived. Mystery is stripped away.

FLOW

Feedback shapes original knowledge sources.

We have moved from hierarchical to network. It is end user driven. A right decision today may not be right tomorrow.

In a knowledge economy, the flow of knowledge is the equivalent of the oil pipe in an industrial economy. Creating, preserving, and utilizing knowledge flow should be a key organizational activity.

Knowledge flow can be likened to a river that meanders through the ecology of an organization. In certain areas, the river pools and in other areas it ebbs. The health of the learning ecology of the organization depends on effective nurturing of flow.

How then does knowledge flow within a network (keeping in mind our discussion that networks may be internal (neural) or external (nodes we have connected) see p.29)? Which factors impact the process? If we tentatively ascribe life-like properties to our learning networks, we can partly answer this challenge. Any living organism seeks two primary functions: replication and preservation. Nodes within our networks follow similar aspirations. Established beliefs and learning often ensure that new information is routed through the existing network. New information is evaluated and coded reflective of the existing learning network.

A simple illustration: if one believes that people cannot be trusted, the activities of those around will be interpreted through this framework (routed through our neural network and coded with meaning reflective of this larger view). Meaning is attached as an *add-on* to the knowledge source, ensuring that the existing network replicates itself. If the entire network is subsequently reconfigured according to a new meme, the knowledge itself stays, but the meaning is reconfigured.

In a similar sense, when knowledge is introduced to a learning network that is contradictory to the established structur, the existing network, in an effort to preserve itself, attempts to route around or push the new node to the fringe. This results in limited connections being formed, and as a result, the new node does not gain significant status with the larger network. If the node does acquire a certain level of status, new knowledge may route through the node, permitting the node to begin replicating itself, encoding meaning to knowledge. Consider the implications when we acquire new understanding about a subject matter.

The text you are reading presents a certain context game—a manner of seeing the world. As a reader, you may find some concepts enlightening and adopt them as key attributes of how you view knowledge. Other concepts may not be relevant or insightful. Relevant concepts will form a pathway that will route (explain) new ideas and knowledge.

FLOW INHIBITORS are elements internal to a network that reduce the possibility of information and knowledge flow. This might include elements like biases or preconceived notions. Our own cognition and emotions can be legitimate flow inhibitors. External inhibitors also impact the flow of information between learners. The physical design of a space, the bureaucracy, or knowledge-sharing culture of an environment, will influence and determine how well knowledge flows between networks.

FLOW ACCELERATORS are elements and conditions inherent in a network that permit the rapid formation and distribution of knowledge. Receptivity and motivation are two key accelerators. External attributes of an ecology or network also influence how well knowledge flows.

A culture of openness, recognized value of cooperation, and tools and time allotted for collaboration all contribute to accelerate network formation.

Spaces and Structures of Knowledge

Today's big companies do very little to enhance the productivity of their professionals. In fact, their vertically oriented organization structures, retrofitted with ad hoc and matrix overlays, nearly always make professional work more complex and inefficient.

Lowell Bryan and Claudia Joyce[80]

Spaces and structures are the organizational elements of society. We dialogue and function within these elements. Spaces—schools, online, museums, corporate boardrooms—provide the environment in which we do our conversing, meeting, knowledge sharing, and dialoguing. Structures—classification systems, hierarchies, command and control, libraries, government—provide the process and manner in which decisions are made, knowledge flows, and things get done.

Structures and spaces direct affordances. New structural approaches permit the formation of organizations prepared to manage diverse and rapid knowledge growth. Building a baseball diamond enables competitive baseball (or an impromptu soccer game). Creating a concert hall permits performances and concerts.

Our corporate structures generate product-based affordances. Is this what is needed in our era today? *It is time to restructure our structures to ensure more relevant connections with the nature of knowledge today.* What affordances do we seek: innovation, adaptability, holistic actions, systems-view perception, tolerance of chaos, emergence, and self-formation?

Instead of being designed and controlled through central means, a distributed structure generates outcomes through the act of self-organization.

What are the spaces and structures of knowledge today?

What should a business look like? How should an organization function? How should we make decisions? Manage our resources? Achieve our strategies?

Ecologies and **networks** provide the solution to needed structures and spaces to house and facilitate knowledge flow.

Knowledge Spaces
The place in which knowledge occurs

Static and Linear

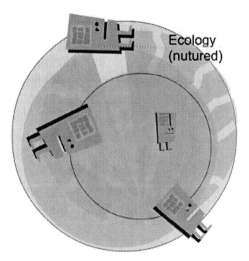

Ecology
(nutured)

Figure 34. Knowledge Spaces

Spaces are themselves agents for change.
Changed spaces will change practice.[81]

Ecologies permit diverse, multi-faceted concepts…and meaning to emerge based on how items are organized or self-organize. Ecologies are capable of managing rapid growth, adapting to new competition, differing perspectives, and enabling innovative concepts and ideas to gain traction.

An ecology, a knowledge sharing environment, should have the following components:[82]

Informal, . The system should not define the learning and
Not Structured   discussion that happens. The system should be flexible enough to allow participants to create according to their needs.

Tool-Rich . . Many opportunities for users to dialogue and connect. Video, audio, text, face to face. Too much choice, however is not always desirable, as it can overwhelm the end-user.[83]

Consistency and Time	New communities, projects and ideas start with much hype and promotion and then slowly fade. To create a knowledge -haring ecology, participants need to see consistent activity.
Trust	High, social contact (face-to-face or online) is needed to foster a sense of trust and comfort. Secure and safe environments are critical for trust to develop.
Simplicity	Other characteristics need to be balanced with the need for simplicity. Great ideas fail because of complexity in expression. Simple, social approaches are often most effective. The selection of tools and the creation of the community structure should reflect this need for simplicity.
Decentralized, Fostered, Connected	Instead of centralized, managed, and isolated, the ecology should allow individuals to define and form connections, functioning as separate nodes in an aggregated whole.
High tolerance for experimentation and failure	Innovation is a function of experimentation, accidents, and failure. To foster knowledge growth, innovation, and sharing, organizational processes must be supported by an environment of tolerance and a spirit of inquiry.

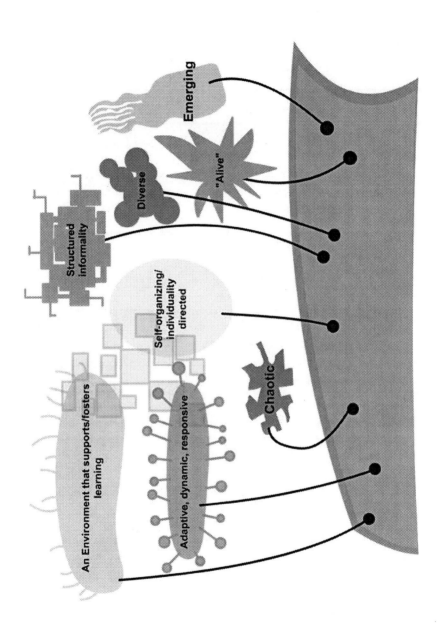

Figure 35. Learning and Knowledge Ecology

These ecologies possess numerous characteristics that need to be attended to in the design process. The following are required in an effective ecology:

> ▷ a space for gurus and beginners to connect,
> ▷ a space for self-expression,
> ▷ a space for debate and dialogue,
> ▷ a space to search archived knowledge,
> ▷ a space to learn in a structured manner,
> ▷ a space to communicate new information and knowledge indicative of changing elements within the field of practice (news, research), and
> ▷ a space to nurture ideas, test new approaches, prepare for new competition, pilot processes.

Ecologies are nurtured and fostered…instead of constructed, organized, and mandated.

An ecology provides the special formations needed by organizations. Ecologies are: loose, free, dynamic, adaptable, messy, and chaotic. Innovation does not arise through hierarchies. As a function of creativity, innovation requires trust, openness, and a spirit of experimentation—where random ideas and thoughts can collide for re-creation.

But corporations require structure, consistent functioning, clear outcomes. Ecologies and corporations repel, because processes have been crafted that favor structure at the expense of innovation and creativity. We seek certainty instead of opportunity.

How can organizations adopt ecologies when their goal is to drive out chaos and messiness (not embrace it)?

Beyond a change of organizational mindset (which would not hurt), networks provide the new structural model. The cause-effect, top-down, mandated flow of hierarchies is replaced with the emergent, loosely connected, adaptive model of networks.

***Hierarchy** adapts knowledge to the organization;*
***a network** adapts the organization to the knowledge.*

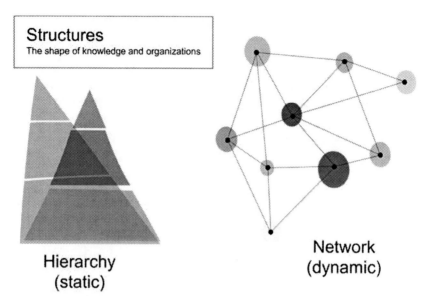

Structures
The shape of knowledge and organizations

Hierarchy
(static)

Network
(dynamic)

Figure 36. Knowledge Structures

Table 2. **Hierarchies and Networks**	
Static	Dynamic
Structured (in advance)	Flowing structure
Stable	Equality (in theory)
Managed	Connected entities
Boundaries	Participant & process-defined structure
Centralized	Decentralized
Certainty	Adaptive
Managed and created	Nurtured and fostered
Pre-filtered	Emergent

The networked world continuously refines, reinvents, and reinterprets knowledge, often in an autonomic manner.

Morris, Mason, Robson, Lefrier, & Collier[84]

Networks occur within ecologies.

Nodes and connectors comprise the structure of a network. In contrast, an ecology is a living organism. It influences the formation of the network itself. For example, each learner in an organization possesses a personal learning network. The health of this network is influenced by the suitability of the ecology in which the learner exists. If the ecology is healthy, it will permit networks to flourish and grow. If the ecology is not healthy, networks will not develop optimally. A healthy knowledge ecology allows individuals to quickly and effectively enhance their existing learning…enabling better decisions…better performance.

DECENTRALIZATION OF KNOWLEDGE

Things fall apart; the Center cannot hold.

William Butler Yeats[85]

Pieces are held everywhere…stitching together reality is in the hands of many.

Marvin Minsky presents intelligence as the function of *"many little parts, each mindless by itself."*[86] When these parts connect or join, they create intelligence. The decentralization of knowledge reverses the joining formed by others (experts, editors) and permits individuals the capacity to connect knowledge in a manner they find useful.

Steven Johnson builds on Minsky's thoughts, and details emergence as *"a network of self-organization, of disparate agents that unwittingly create a higher-level order."*[87] These agents can create diverse structures (ant colonies, brains, cities) through the process of connecting by following simple rules. Does this relate to learning? Is a new entity brought into our cognitive network a "mindless agent"?

Perhaps the bigger opportunity here is to consider the amplification effect of joining individual entities (regardless of whether we classify them as mindless or mindful). Landauer and Dumais tackle the concern of people having *"more knowledge than appears to be present in the information to which they have been exposed."*[88] They suggest that the answer to the "mystery of excessive learning" is found in the "weak interrelations," which exist in certain domains of knowledge. When we bring a new element into the knowledge space, it can serve as an amplifier for knowledge that is currently known, much like Minsky's agents combine to form higher-order intelligence.[89]

Filling a gap in our neural networks creates new pathways.

So what does this have to do with decentralized knowledge?

"Know where" is replacing "know what" and "know how." The rapid, continual knowledge flow cannot be contained and held in the human mind. To survive, we extend ourselves through our networks: computers, humans, databases, and still unfolding new tools.

Our co-workers no longer sit at a different desk. They sit in a different country.

How does theory ("construct in advance") shape knowledge spaces? To what degree should knowledge emerge and influence theory?

Aggregation of knowledge/information sources has really changed over the last few years. Until recently, most of our information was delivered through a centering agent—a television, newspaper, magazine, or radio. In this model, our primary task was to absorb or consume the structure of information created by a third party.

The centering agents have come undone. Knowledge agents continue to connect and form, but not according to the views of others. We have become active organizers of individual agents. We weave our networks.

> *But I thought you said that our role was one*
> *of allowing knowledge to emerge?*

True. We wade into the river of knowledge, not to direct its flow to a predefined purpose, but to recognize the patterns that are emerging and to base our actions on changed context and characteristics of knowledge.

We no longer exclusively read newspapers or watch the evening news. We used to go to one source of information to get a thousand points of information. Now, we go to a thousand sources of information to create our one view. We have become the filter, mediator, and the weaver. Aggregation amplifies knowledge and learning.

While this process is effective on many levels, it has its challenges. Going to one source of information is much simpler than attempting to consume many different elements. It is less stressful. It requires less thought and foraging for needed knowledge. Questions of validity and trust are answered with each information source (at least until a relationship has been developed).

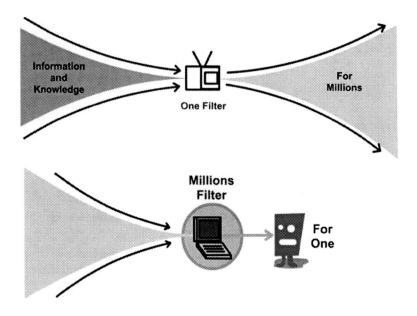

Figure 37. Filters

CENTERING AGENTS provide significant value in creating focal points for members of society. These agents serve a diverse base and are structured to provide appeal to many different individuals (race, religion, politics). People of different political stripes, for example, are able to dialogue because of the common language and understanding created by centering agents.

What happens when we no longer share centering agents?

What happens when all of my information comes only from sources that promote view points I already hold?

It is easier to access…and to ignore diverse viewpoints. This process is creating a serious divide in the ability of people to dialogue and share common understandings. We can now listen only to perspectives already in line with our own. The breakdown of common understanding and dialogue poses a risk to the civility of society. The moderating influence of diversity is not prominent when we can shape our dialogue spaces to suit our views. Accidental diversity must now give way to intentional diversity. We must seek the viewpoints of others to create a unified whole.

It is to our health that we consume information from differing spectrums of thought. Whatever our view or perspective, as actors on a global stage, we need to move (at minimum) to dialogue with those around us.

Closing spaces equals closing minds.

Clear aims through **decentralized means** is **THE** challenge for organizations today. Organizations need to achieve goals, objectives, targets, but they need to achieve them in non-linear ways. The assumption that control determines outcome is a mindset that was questionable in the industrial era…and laughable in the knowledge era.

Even when we understand the value of decentralization, the familiarity of centralized and controlled processes and outcomes are impediments. In the end, the appeal of control often exceededs the prospect of value from decentralization. The misleading, and false assumption of many leaders is: "How can I make sure that things are happening the way I want them to?" It presupposes control as a requirement for effective functioning.

Are you saying that all centralization is ineffective?

Absolutely not. Centralization is effective when matched to the appropriate task. In our earlier discussion of learning, we pursued holistic models in order to attend to the diverse and complex nature of learning. No one single model meets the needs of all possible situations. Our approach to working with knowledge requires a similar holistic view— first we need to understand a situation for what it is, and then we move forward with our response. Centralization is not always the answer. Neither is decentralization.

We have a mindset of "knowing before application." We feel that new problems must be tamed by our previous experience. When we encounter a challenge, we visit our database of known solutions with the objective of applying a template solution on the problem. Many organizations are not comfortable with suspending judgment. The moment a problem takes an initial known shape, the solutions begin to flow.

The act of labeling is an attempt to provide order where order does not exist (at least in the mind of the listener). Labeling is a cognitive off-loading process; once we can put someone or a concept into a box, we do not have to be as active in making meaning. Instead, we can rely on memory to provide meaning and understanding. While natural, it is the root of much harm—racism, prejudice, and misunderstanding.

The assumption that order does not exist unless we enforce it, is false. We feel that we must sufficiently grapple with an idea or situation until we have *extracted* value or meaning. It is difficult to accept that order and meaning can emerge on its own. Chaos, we feel, requires our hand for order. Randomness may conceal order, and acting too quickly may result in missing the true meaning.

…and yet…

the pinnacle of human activity is one of order making—cities, societies, books, vehicles, buildings. *We are order-makers.* Perhaps in today's complex knowledge space, our role of order-making requires periods of suspension, where we assess knowledge first (for what it is) and apply order second (once we know the characteristics of the entity we are ordering).

Instead of trying to force the new nature of knowledge into organizational structures, let it exist for a while. See what happens. Do not decide the entire solution in advance. See the process as more of a dance than a structured enactment of a solution. React as the environment adjusts. Allow feedback to shape the final product. Let the process bring its own lessons before applying structured approaches. Perhaps the real value exists in the knowledge patterns that emerge.

Centralizing decentralized processes results in killing the value inherent in decentralization. Relaxing on control is vital for sustained knowledge growth, innovation, sharing, and dissemination. Centralization works well for organized knowledge or established structures. Decentralization is effective when things change rapidly, diverse viewpoints are required, and knowledge has not settled into a "knowable, defined" state.

The views that we must know before we can do, and that problems require clear solutions, can be limiting in certain instances (especially instances of high complexity or uncertainty).

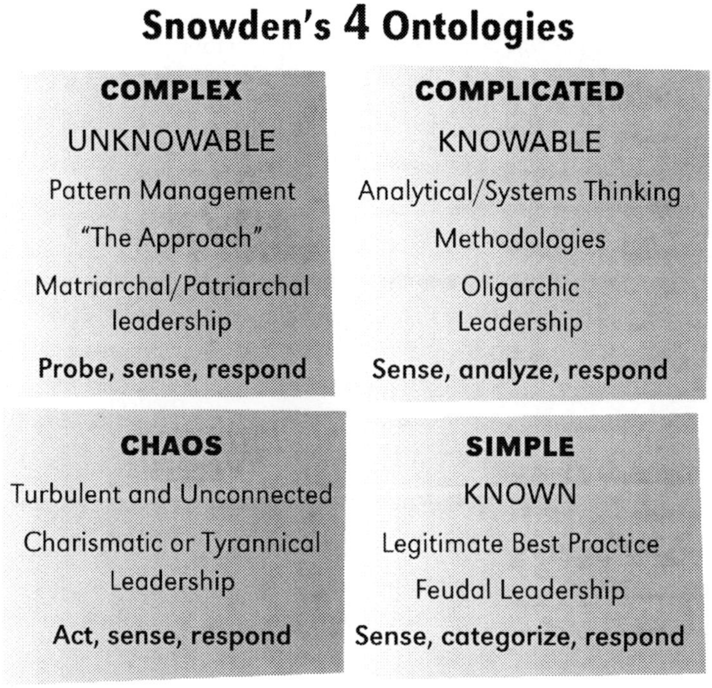

Snowden's 4 Ontologies

COMPLEX	COMPLICATED
UNKNOWABLE	KNOWABLE
Pattern Management	Analytical/Systems Thinking
"The Approach"	Methodologies
Matriarchal/Patriarchal leadership	Oligarchic Leadership
Probe, sense, respond	**Sense, analyze, respond**
CHAOS	**SIMPLE**
Turbulent and Unconnected	KNOWN
Charismatic or Tyrannical Leadership	Legitimate Best Practice
	Feudal Leadership
Act, sense, respond	**Sense, categorize, respond**

Figure 38. Snowden's Ontology[90]

Knowing often arises in the process of doing. Solutions are contained within the problems themselves (not external, templated responses), and problems always morph as we begin to work on them. As Snowden indicates, different situations present themselves at different levels of clarity. Some elements are knowable...others are complex. The nature of the situation determines our response. We cannot effectively impose order on chaotic or complex spaces. Instead, we must probe and sense.

> If the only Tool you have is a **Hammer**,
> you tend to see every Problem as a **Nail**.
>
> Abraham Maslow[91]

The real value of a new tool is not the tool itself.

It is what the tool enables.

A hammer is not only useful for hitting nails. Obviously that is the task at its most basic, but what does it mean? In the case of the hammer, it means we can build a doghouse, a bookshelf, or a house.

Until we look past the task and functionality of a tool—to what the tool enables—we largely miss the beauty of why it is so useful.

But understanding the tool is only part of the challenge. We must also understand the nature of the task in which we are engaged. First we see the task. Then we select the tool. Then we adjust and acquire new tools (and processes) as the experience warrants.

We often apply our thinking at the wrong stage—we think planning is the key, but fail to recognize that the rapid pace of knowledge development is moving more emphasis to adapting during the process. Business and learning are not about following a map or preplanned route. Functioning in a knowledge stream is a give-and-take experience with the environment and factors that arise.

Tools and approaches possess, in themselves, innate attributes for optimal function (saw for cutting wood, hammer for building).

Books, like the one you are reading, are most often a one-sided view of the knowledge of a particular space (and, in certain fields, they can be dated by the time they are published). *Content is something that is created in the process of learning, not only in advance of learning.*

Affordance

Each tool possesses inherent traits that will determine use. Task is to have access to a broad range of tools to adjust to situation.

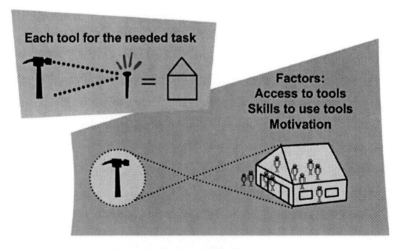

Figure 39. Tools and Affordances

Content is the codification of our knowledge, our art, our vision, our dreams, and our aspirations. As little as five years ago, content came pre-packaged. You could get your content fix in the form of a textbook, a CD, a newscast, a newspaper, or a classroom.

We can now acquire our resources in any manner that we desire. We are re-packagers. Learners weave together (connect) various content and conversation elements to create an integrated, though at times contradictory, network of issues and concerns. We take pieces, add pieces, dialogue, reframe, rethink, connect, and ultimately, we end up with some type of pattern that symbolizes what is happening "out there" and what it means to us.

Learning and knowing occur in networks and ecologies, not hierarchical, pre-organized structures.
The central filtering agent is no longer the newspaper, teacher, manager, or institution. It is the INDIVIDUAL.
Think about what that means to our organizations today.
It changes everything.

The center has broken apart in other industries—movies, music, software; we can expect knowledge and learning will not be immune.

What does it mean to us?

What should we be doing now to prepare our institutions?

Ourselves?

Knowledge is about a certain type of organization. When the capacity to organize is in the hands of others, we are passive consumers.

When we ourselves organize (re-package), we become knowledge **conduits,** not **containers.**

People do not want to visit your content. They want to pull your content into their sites, programs, or applications. Sense-making needs to happen in their context. This is a profound change.

We are still fixated on the notion of content. We think we are making great concessions when we give individuals control, and start to see them as co-creators. That misses the essence of the change: individuals want control of their space. They want to create the ecology in which they function and learn.

Sense-making happens in their context. Today, it is about pulling content from numerous sites and allowing the individual to repurpose it in the format they prefer (allowing them to create/recognize patterns). Much like the music industry had to learn that people do not want to pay for a whole album when all they want is one song, content providers (education, museums, and libraries) need to see the end user does not want the entire experience—they want only the pieces they want.

Dialogue and learning will happen on their time, in their space, on their device. We must create the ecology that allows for maximum innovation, so that the greatest number of recombinations are possible.

Does anyone actually DO this stuff, or do people like you just theorize?

One of the most obvious learning ecologies is the **INTERNET** itself. It is a wonderful example of a space where we can learn from experts, informally, formally, or in communities.

> *Didn't you do away with experts in your discussion of how end-users now have access and control?*

Experts do provide a valuable role and source of guidance. Holistic perspectives are important. Context games create a loose structure to a conversation, but fail to capture an entire perspective. As an author, in order to make useful statements such as *"Knowledge is now at the disposal of the many,"* I leave things unsaid *(but experts play a key role, and when experts are the focus of the discussion, I will attend to their role)*. Thorough context games—as an effort to eliminate misunderstandings—are time consuming. When we dialogue, it is in relation to something—to an event, a person, or some situation before us.

When we take one approach, we are leaving many other factors unattended, but impacted. When we pursue knowledge on one level, we are making choices that change things. But that choice does not happen in a vacuum. Other parts of our organization will also need to change. It is important to be aware of what we are leaving behind in our choices... and that one view *(systems thinking is* useful *in determining interconnection of actions)* does not lead to universal application *(systems thinking should be used for* everything*)*.

This one-dimensional view is lazy thinking. Each tool provides affordances for certain tasks. To advocate for social technologies (or informal learning), is not to deem all hierarchy as irrelevant. It is relevant…but not in all situations and for all tasks. Hierarchies have a role, but at a much diminished level…and always within the appropriate context.

CHOICE = DESELECTION.

When we pursue one direction, we are saying no to many others. What we do not choose is often as important as what we do choose. We need to look at where the energy is expended, not where it is solidified.

Categorizing offloads cognition to established views—but what are the costs?

When we rely on outdated knowledge (due to classification in advance of all elements being known), we encounter inaccurate information, wrong judgments, and un-acknowledged changed foundations

Even the images and proposed ways of looking at knowledge provided in this book are an attempt to provide some organization. How can we act if we do not solidify knowledge—even slightly? Often, our action for volatile, rapidly changing knowledge needs to be one of waiting for patterns to emerge. The most effective model for categorization and classification is the one that **enables the greatest potential** for connection, recombination, diversity, knowledge to speak for itself, and situations and elements to emerge according to their characteristics, not our organizational schema.

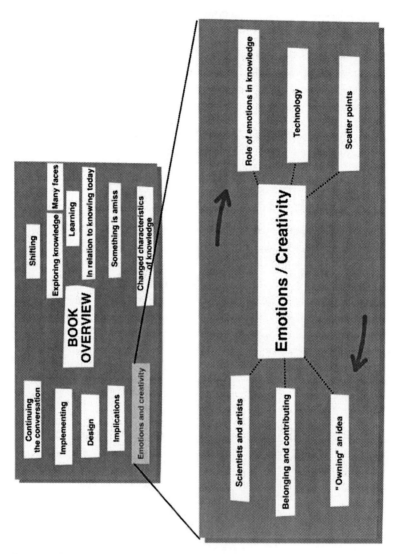

Figure 40. Emotions

EMOTIONS & CREATIVITY

We exist in multiple domains. We have spent centuries attempting to understand cognitive, physical, and spiritual domains. The emotional space of life has been relegated to the status of inconvenient. What role do emotions play in knowledge creation and dissemination? The error of assuming we exist only in one space at a time—for example, that we are logical, without emotional influence—results in ineffective views of knowledge.

We do not function according to formulas and rules. We exist in a rich interplay of multiple domains, expressed as context games…where our emotions, desires, and logic are expressed in dialogue and debate with others. The way in which we interact with knowledge is influenced by our emotions. We are at times, unwilling (even unable) to see views and perspectives that are not aligned with our own. The use of logic as a tool for swaying opinions is ineffective when core beliefs are challenged.

> Emotion is messy, complicated, primitive, and undefined
> because it's all over the place,
> intertwined with cognition and physiology.
>
> John J. Ratey[92]

How are emotions to be rightly perceived to the overall process of knowledge? What are the emotional factors involved in learning and knowledge acquisition/creation?

What about the beautiful things of life: love, justice, truth, honor? Our noble desires to shape a better world, when our contribution of time and effort goes against "the invisible hand"[93] of self-interest?

We advance humanity's potential through **knowledge**. We advance humanity through **emotion**.

But what of the higher good? What of our quest to be more…to be beyond humanity? What are the narratives that we are serving today?

Is it true that:

> Without a narrative, life has no meaning.
> Without meaning, learning has no purpose.
> Neil Postman[94]

What is the greater purpose of being human?

What about faith?

God and *technology*. God and *humanity*. God and *knowledge*.

What are we to make of these? What are these to make of us?

How do we aspire to the higher good of life while engaged in the daily flow? How can we retreat to reflect, meditate, pray?

> **Technology is an exacting master.**
> **Ever requiring more, promising hope anew.**

Or does technology make us more human? A grandparent video-chatting with a grandchild. A granddaughter teaching her grandfather how to navigate the web. A student learning from an expert a thousand miles away. A community formed through need, not geography.

Perhaps the question is not about technology. It is about us.

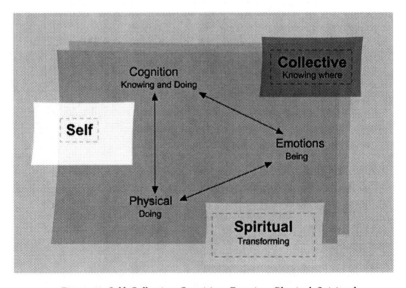

Figure 41. Self, Collective, Cognition, Emotion, Physical, Spiritual

Great are they who see that spiritual is stronger than any material force, that thoughts rule the world.

Ralph Waldo Emerson[95]

Emotions influence our ability to see knowledge. They act as gatekeepers to our neural network. Logic cannot begin unless emotions are held in balance.

Knowledge pace outruns our ability to capture, hold, and analyze. We hit a scatter point.

DO WE:

Accept chaos and ambiguity?

or

Desire to maintain control? (which in turn requires more complex structures of organization)

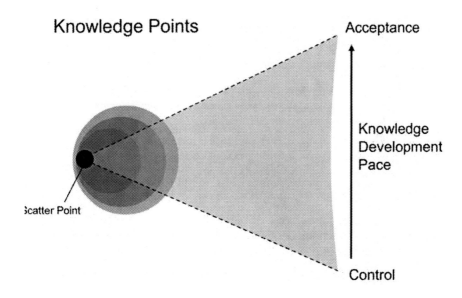

Figure 42. Scatter Point of Coping

We exist in dimensions beyond pure cognition. We are shaped by social interactions. We are influenced by our emotions, our motivations. We require transformative (spiritual) knowledge for novel recombinations (to rethink and recast information).

Contentment will not come through knowledge. Knowledge is like an errant appetite with short satiation. What is the missing piece? Or is the angst-filled pursuit of knowledge the nature of our existence?

There is something rewarding about having an idea—owning it, being recognized for it. Even when we share, we attach identity to what we have created. In creating knowledge, we experience life, identity, hope. To contribute to the public space, to be recognized, to be a part of something bigger—these motivations drive us.

We want to belong. We want to be a part of the many, but only if we are ourselves. We do not want to fade and cease to exist as we meld with the crowd. Our tools are about individualization and personalization, but we individualize so we are a (unique) part of the crowd.

We answer questions differently at different times because we are in different connection-forming (or neural pathway) states. We still possess the same key traits and concerns, but we see the network structure from a different relational dimension.

Context shapes our actions, our beliefs, our morality. This is not to say that it is right. It just is. We are different people at work, at home, at a ball game, with parents, with friends, with co-workers.

Pascal has apparently stated that "*all of man's problems stem from his inability to sit in a quiet room alone.*"[96] In a learning sense, we have a similar challenge. It seems that we will utilize any tool of distraction to prevent a "quieting of our minds." Save a few minutes by using a search engine, spend more time searching other resources. Save time by having technology manage part of our knowledge, immediately set out to experience even more.

Learning has a reflective component. Most people will trust a bad idea they read in a book sooner than a good idea they arrive at through reasoning and reflection. Our restlessness is a challenge to learning. We rarely slow down enough to begin to use our advanced thinking skills. Instead we skim the surface of knowledge, learning to distrust our own intuition and cognition.

When a learner sits down and thinks, she/he is engaging in a reflective process. Nebulous thoughts and feelings are put to words. External ideas are scrutinized. The natural capacity of harmonizing our emotions and thoughts with ideas and concepts is evoked—a small cognitive and emotional oasis in the desert of busyness, and, I imagine more learning occurs in only a few minutes here than hours anywhere else...

But perhaps more importantly, the focus on utility and conve-
nience distracts us from questions of greater significance. If
our ability to cope with future crises depends upon our reflec-
tive depth, our powers of self-recollection, our inner quiet, our
ability to invest a few words with profundity rather than many
words with shallowness, our sensitivity to the subtle qualities
of things and not merely their superficial logic—well, then, we
have to recognize that the ease with which we commandeer
unrooted and decontextualized "information" from all sides
can be as much a distractive threat as a ground for hope.

Steve Talbott[97]

Daniel Pink[98] suggests that we are moving from an age defined by logic to an age defined by creativity. Creativity is the ability to see *"new associations between existing ideas or concepts"[99]*...and to bring new realities into being. Creativity involves the ability to form, reform, create, breakdown, and rebuild.

The creativity of children (as parents can attest) comes from their willingness to put things together and take them apart, to blur contexts (does this item belong here or there?) and to engage items for what they are (not how they have been defined in advance).

Our organizational activities (whether instructing students, or conducting a business meeting) are dominated by structure and consistency. *Creativity dies in those environments.* Creativity, as random play, requires an environment of trust.

Why is creativity important today? The process of creativity (connections, sense-making, creation, re-creation) is very much like the characteristics of knowledge and learning today (see connectivism, page 16).

Scientist versus Artist

"What is the evidence?" is prominent question when discussing knowledge and learning approaches. Evidence in this case is almost always defined empirically (scientifically). What is the Return on Investment (ROI)? Where is the magic and beauty? Are empirical measurements of learning our only option?

It is important to understand and measure (though measurement should extend beyond simple dollars) the impact of training and learning. Unfortunately, the *scientists of learning* have the dominant voice in the learning space. The artists are not being heard.

The scientist's role is one of determining best approaches to knowledge discovery, creation, and dissemination (through empirical research, qualitative and quantitative analysis). What is the role of the artist (or more broadly, creativity) in the learning space?

The artist is the individual who sees the magic in learning. They may not know exactly why something worked well, but can see (and dare I say, feel?) that the learners are changing, growing, and developing. The artist of learning sees beauty in the dialogue, in the interaction, in the connections formed between what is known and what is becoming known. The artist sees (and accepts) the beauty of uncertainty and values learning as both a process and a product. In creating a knowledge environment, the artist splashes the magic of learning across the entire canvas of life. Tools are used like paint brushes to create the desired painting of learning.

We need the voices of both the scientist and the artist. Neither one is necessarily better than the other. In some cases, a business may require the metrics and method of a clearly-defined, scientific model. In other cases (especially when pursuing innovation and creativity), they may desire the beauty of learning created by the artist. **Both,** held in balance and for the appropriate task, are needed for learning and knowledge sharing.

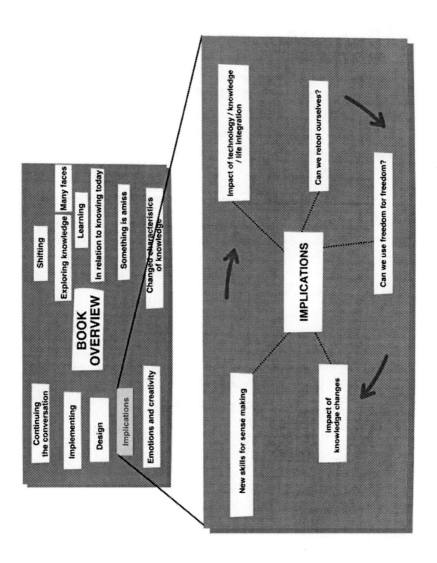

Figure 43. Implications

IMPLICATIONS...
STRUCTURAL/SPATIAL IMPACT

Society, community, family are all conserving institutions. They try to maintain stability, and to prevent, or at least to slow down, change. But the organization of the post-capitalist society of organizations is a destabilizer. Because its function is to put knowledge to work—on tools, processes, and products; on work; on knowledge itself—it must be organized for constant change.

Peter F. Drucker[100]

What does it mean to have technology tightly integrated with life? Our tools are extensions of ourselves.[101] We desire to extend our competence by creating tools that cover our weaker attributes. What happens when we stand at the doorway to re-wiring humanity? What happens when we become integrated (implanted) with technology?

What becomes of our humanness? We are entering an era where science, technology, and biology will push at the boundaries of our conceptions of being human. Capacity to do runs ahead of our understanding of implications. The morality that has shaped human knowledge is replaced by the raw urge to KNOW. Pragmatics and possibility reign.

What are the human costs?
FREEDOM?
SANITY?

Can an entire species retool itself as rapidly as new technology requires? We are no longer driving technology. Technology is driving our race. Our challenge exists on a continuum anchored by two point: (a) **keep up** or (b) **resist** and provide alternatives. Morality and ethical discussions are trailing behind progress of science and technology.

Tight human and technology integration. Prophetic declarations of new utopias. New solutions. New realities. To date these have disappointed.

Will technology be different?

Technology simultaneously permits increased individual control and power, while enabling more complex control/surveillance.

The nervous system carries pain and pleasure through the same receptors. Decentralization opens doors for centralization.

Do we have the wisdom to use freedom for freedom?[102]

What is the impact of changes to knowledge?

Overload of Quantity. . We can no longer manage the quantity of knowledge ourselves. We cope by relying on networks of people and technology.

Overload of Diversity. . Knowing resides in the collective of many differing, diverse viewpoints. This requires new skills of interacting and functioning, especially since our schools are still teaching basics for an era that no longer exists.

Skills Outdated. . The skills that have served us well for navigating hierarchical, structured knowledge no longer serve our needs. We require sensing skills (to sense what is happening, how things are changing)…and improved capacity to respond/react.

Dehumanizing. . We have yet to learn how to be human in this space. We need to learn how to communicate our emotions (empathy, courtesy) in virtual spaces.

Validation/Authenticity . . How is authority created? How do we know who we can trust? How do we know an idea has value? Is the validation of peers in a distributed environment as significant as the validation of knowledge through established models by experts?

Identity. . What is happening with identity? How do I know you are who you say you are? …third-party voices can speak into the process; they can validate and comment on our authority and identity.

To misjudge the velocity and ferocity of change is to risk obsolescence. Today, more rapidly than any era, kingdoms rise and fall. Prominent corporations experience competitive pressures from corporations in previously consumer-only countries. Adaptation is constant.

Attempting to do more of what has been done in the past is not the answer. We need to do **new things in new ways.** It makes little sense to become more efficient in things that serve yesterday's model.

Organizations are awakening to a changed world—they sense it, but the language is still ensconced in the mindset of hierarchy and control. New technology is still applied in traditional means—with the intent to manage, control, and direct activities or outcomes.

The desire for centralization is strong. Organizations want people to access their sites for content/interaction/knowledge. People, on the other hand, already have their personal online spaces. As a customer, they want to experience your company through their medium. As an employee, they want to experience your company through their larger identity.

The desire to control and manage communities expresses the view that control equates to better prospects of achieving intended outcomes, is evident. Communities have traditionally been conceptualized to function in hierarchical structures—pockets of innovation (with horizontal industry/intra-industry connections) in structured environments.

When we try to create communities online, we take the same approach— come to our community. The community should come to the user. The true value in the conversations is the connections formed between individuals. *Essentially, a community is a connection-forming space.*

Most individuals have created a scattered identity and presence. I have pieces of my thoughts scattered across numerous articles, website, podcasts, and presentations. I do not really want to join a community. I want the connection values of communities to be available to me in my own online space and presence.

Today, communities are about end-user control. We still achieve centralized aims (dialogue about learning and technology), but we do so through decentralized means.

We like to make decisions on "what is known"—what is the skillset required when knowledge moves too fast? We make decisions by sensing, not by knowing in advance.

Complexity corrodes clear paths…we now hold things in suspended states until more is revealed.

Do we aspire to certainty as an end? How can we function when our choices are not based on certainty, but instead on a *"best shot"* view of the space?

What types of skills do our learners need?[103]

Anchoring . . .	Staying focused on important tasks while undergoing a deluge of distractions.
Filtering . . .	Managing knowledge flow and extracting important elements.
Connecting with Each Other . . .	Building networks in order to continue to stay current and informed.
Being Human Together . . .	Interacting at a human, not only utilitarian, level...to form social spaces.
Creating and Deriving Meaning . . .	Understanding implications, comprehending meaning and impact.
Evaluation and Authentication . . .	Determining the value of knowledge... and ensuring authenticity.
Altered Processes of Validation . . .	Validating people and ideas within appropriate context.
Critical and Creative Thinking . . .	Question and dreaming.
Pattern Recognition . . .	Recognizing patterns and trends.
Navigate Knowledge Landscape . . .	Navigating between repositories, people, technology, and ideas while achieving intended purposes.
Acceptance of Uncertainty . . .	Balancing what is known with the unknown... to see how existing knowledge relates to what we do not know.
Contextualizing (understanding context games) . . .	Understanding the prominence of context... seeing continuums...ensuring key contextual issues are not overlooked in context-games.

Now that we have seen things "break apart,"
we need better ways of putting them back together.

How do we achieve larger-scale societal understandings, if we are all creating our personal structures?

How do we pull the pieces together? We are scattered across physical and virtual worlds. Our knowledge sources are global (and constant). How do we blend our knowledge-seeking activities? How much do we rely on technology to seek and present knowledge for our use?

We need new skills and tools. We have duplicated the functioning of physical activities in the virtual space. Our encyclopedias and archives mirror physical properties of knowledge. We need tools that permit us to step into the knowledge stream and capture points of interest for immediate use and future reference, and a connection to inform us if the knowledge source itself has changed. We need the ability to capture and express our knowledge in a manner that permits others to see "what we are all about." The capacity for shared understanding today does not arise from being exposed to the same resources. *It arises from being transparent with each other.* A tool is required that allows us to manage our identity and share what we wish with those we wish.

The cognitive load of functioning without boundaries (networks or frameworks) is intense. We require the skills and a means to make sense in order to keep up with how knowledge flows today. We used to make sense through newspapers, books, and journals. How is sense-making different when it occurs through numerous, small, often-unconnected experiences?

The greater the amount of information, the more the value point shifts from the information itself, and on to structures that permit the creation, dissemination, validation, access, co-creation, and use of knowledge (as presented in Figure 3).

Figure 44. Designing

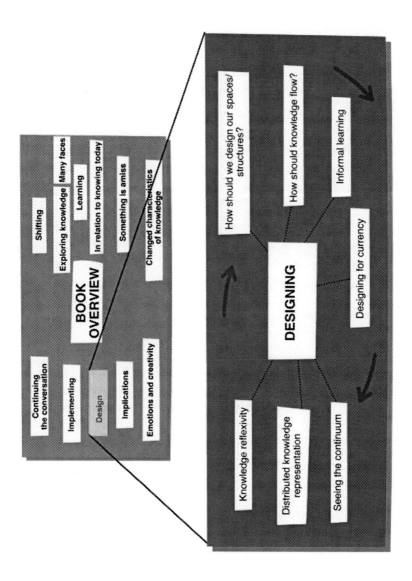

DESIGNING

*Businesses are themselves
a form of design. The design of a business
encompasses its strategy, organizational structure,
management processes, culture, and a host of other factors.
Business designs evolve over time through a process of
differentiation, selection, and amplification, with the market
as the ultimate arbi ter of fitness…the three-way co-
evolution of physical technologies, social technologies, and
business designs…accounts for the patterns of change and
growth we see in the economy.*

Eric Beinhocker[104]

How should we design our organizations to align with the changed
context and characteristics of knowledge?

The design of organizations should permit the creation and distribution
of value. In the industrial era, value was defined by the transport of raw
goods to factories, which created the final products. Organizations were
created to permit effective flow of goods. As physical entities, hierarchy
permitted optimal flow and planning. Knowledge, today's value point,
requires we suitably redesign our organizations. We need to permit effective flow and utilization of knowledge.

When we focus on designing ecologies in which people can forage for
knowledge, we are less concerned about communicating the minutiae
of changing knowledge. Instead, we are creating the conduit through
which knowledge will flow. What is the difference between our current
organizational designs and networks and ecologies?

We have designed our corporations for stability. Planning cycles, bud-
geting, strategic goals, mission statements—all operate from an assumption of knowledge as a stable entity.

Our organizations should not be stable. They should be adaptable[105]—

able to react and respond to core changes in a field or society. They should change and morph as required. An ecology is dynamic, rich, and continually evolving. The entire system reacts to changes—internal or external.

Functioning at this level requires adherence to the following principles:

Transparency. . . . Decision processes need to be clear and detailed, allowing others to join in the conversation. Have open conversations. Allow criticism, but answer honestly.

Diversity. . . . Opinions and viewpoints from broad perspectives need to be available. Gain enough information to see as much of the picture as possible.

Distribution. . . . Decision making happens across the network. of Decisions Let nodes in the know make decisions that impact their functioning. Bring decision making as close to the point of impact as possible. If front-line staff will be impacted by a policy, involve them.

Suspend. . . . Knowledge is able to present itself as is, rather Knowledge than forcing into pre-formed containers. Hardening Resist the urge to classify prematurely or to approach new knowledge exclusively through existing containers of knowing.

What does a corporate or organizational ecology and network structure look like? It balances content with context and conduits. Instead of seeking to make decisions based on what is known with certainty, decisions are made much like a diagnosis or therapy. What is currently known drives decision making, but the decisions are like hypotheses.
The capacity for core conditions to change, thereby altering the validity of the decision, drives awareness.

The ecology fosters connections to original and knowledge sources, allowing for *currency* (up-to-date). The ecology fosters rich interaction between disparate fields of knowledge, allowing growth and adaptation of ideas and concepts *(the edge)*. Each participant in the ecology pursues his/her own objectives, but within the organized domain of the knowledge of a particular field. After all, some form of learner competence should emerge as a result of existing in the ecology.

NODES (content and people) and CONNECTIONS are the basic elements of a network. An ecology should permit these networks to develop and flourish without hindrance.

Decisions are made in a transparent manner, where knowledge is considered based on:

1. **TYPE:** to know, to do, to be, to know where, to transform (see Fig. 5)
2. **DOMAIN:** physical, social, emotional, spiritual (see Fig. 6)
3. **STATE:** continuum of hard–soft (see Fig. 8)

Once ascertained, the dialogue and debate surrounding the concern should be open and transparent, seeking to include various, diverse viewpoints. A feedback loop needs to be included to allow for ongoing dialogue after a task has been initiated.

Many hands create a vision. Many hands monitor the vision.

NOTHING IS ALL—each for a proper concept and proper implementation. When we let go of solutions in advance, and instead embrace a therapy view of functioning, we discover that many of the problems we encounter are solved simply by seeking to understand. When we understand our solutions, but not the problem, we often intensify the situation. Most of our problem-solving is more about enacting a pre-configured solution. We are more about applying solutions than attending to the nature of the concern before us.

In this environment of chaos and shifting core elements (note the changing fields of media, music, and news), what we know (usually thought of as possession of content-based knowledge) is replaced with how we continue to stay current and informed.

ENGAGE THE SITUATION. What is it? How does it relate to the tools we have based on our experience? Where do our prescribed solutions fail? How do we engage without forcing the situation into our solutions and methods? How do we enable the situation to teach us?

Many organizations do not focus on the value of informal learning.[106] Even companies who are advanced in this area often do little more than provide software for communities, and try and access the tacit knowledge of others in the organization.

When we have a knowledge need, we often assume that the solution will be found in taking a formal course, but most of our learning is self-organized, not organized by a designer. The most significant skills we possess are acquired through trial, error, and experimentation.

We learn foundational elements through courses…but we innovate through our own learning.

Informal learning is too important to leave to chance.

Why do we not have theories that provide guidelines to designing in these environments? Or is the notion of informal learning too vague (free spirited?) and applying increased design is an effort in futility?

Perhaps the challenge with informal learning is the many different approaches a learner might take (how can we plan and design for it?). Perhaps even our notion of design is worth rethinking—do we design learning? Or do we design environments in which motivated learners can acquire what they need? Yet if we cannot impose some type of order on the process, is it really design? Will corporations invest in a learning theory that is not strongly tied to strategic goals?

Learning is usually viewed as something that happens to a person. A person learns how to solve a physics problem, how to skate, or how to communicate. The assumption is that we are fairly autonomous beings, and that we can acquire within ourselves what we need to know to do the things we want to do. This model works well in areas where one can know everything within a field of knowledge. The model breaks apart as complexity and abundance of knowledge increases. For many, this is a very real problem today. It feels that we simply can not stay on top of our own fields. Forget trying to stay aware of occurrences in other fields. How do we learn in such an environment?

ABUNDANCE = DYSFUNCTIONALITY in a silo learning model. *Superman's Learning Theory*—the notion that I can know in myself what I need to know—is obsolete today.

Why? Designing learning is a simple example. No one person can be subject matter expert, instructional designer, media specialist, and graphic designer. It takes a combination of specialized skills (connected specialization). Take that concept to more complex fields like medicine, astronomy, physics, or launching a space shuttle. It immediately becomes obvious that we need to create a network to hold the points of knowledge. Our knowledge resides in a network-model. The very act of cognition has social dimensions that exist outside the "skull of an individual."[107] Cognitive processing "may be something whose functioning cuts across the superficial physical boundaries between brain, body, and environment."[108]

The aggregation of network nodes is the learning structure. If any critical nodes are removed from a learning network, the entire organism loses effectiveness.

Learning is evolutionary. It is not an event or end goal. Learning is a process. Our personal network is continually being augmented and enhanced by new nodes and connections.

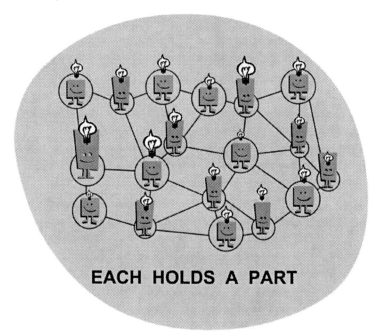

Figure 45. Distributed Knowledge Representation

We are all something, but none of us are everything.

Blaise Pascal[109]

We can not stand alone on our own knowledge. We have to aggregate with other nodes (people, content, knowledge) in order to meet the challenges of a complex information climate. Unfortunately, education (K-12, higher, and corporate) is built on the model that we can fit what is important into one person's head. The network becomes valuable once we combine and connect separate nodes of knowledge.

The **micro** model of how our brain creates connections is represented by the **macro** model of how we create personal learning networks with others.

KNOWLEDGE REFLEXIVITY is a means of ensuring that as the original knowledge source changes, we have a connection which ensures we remain current.[110]

The way most learning is designed today makes this very impractical. The issue stems from the left over remnants of learning design from a society and era of greater stability. But reality has changed for learners. If we take a course, we should have some level of reflexivity for some period of time.

Rather than requiring an employee to continually access a resource to determine if it has changed, an aggregator (pulling knowledge into our spaces)[111] automatically performs the function. It is a time-saving process, but more importantly, ensures that the individual remains current and aware on a particular subject.

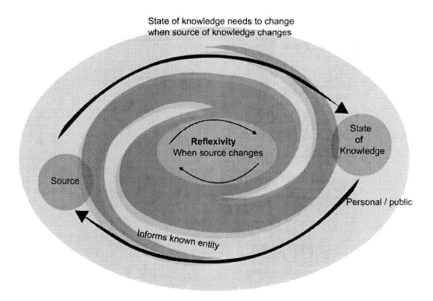

Figure 46. Current Knowledge

Rather than being excited that we can participate in the rich, diverse world of differing perspectives and opinions, we pull back because "we do not know." It is not that we fear the state of not knowing. We fear others seeing that we do not know. How do we teach learners to accept (and value) not knowing?

From an early age, we view "not knowing" as a short coming, rather than a revelation. Perhaps it is in our nature to desire to banish the uncomfortable feelings of not knowing something.

We like clear, black and white, always true answers. We need to step outside of the destination view of learning and embrace the journey view. In many situations the answers do not exist...or they exist, but the context changes so rapidly that we need to continually evaluate what we know and how it applies to what is happening around us.

It is okay to not know. It is healthy to accept confusion as part of the learning and knowledge processes. The presence of certainty is not the aim of knowledge. We often learn most through confusion. It is at the point of confusion that are we actively trying to create connections between varying viewpoints and perspectives. We think critically of new knowledge; we seek to build a neural network that represents the physical/conceptual elements we are encountering...while contrasting those elements with previous experiences and established conceptions.

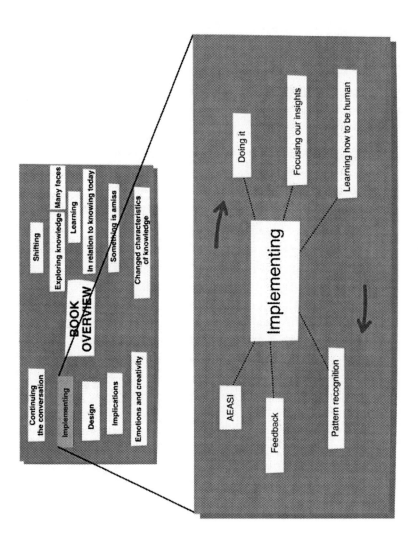

Figure 47. Implementing

IMPLEMENTING

"A little knowledge that acts is worth infinitely more than much knowledge that is idle." Kahlil Gibran[112]

It is not "not knowing" that is the problem. It is the lack of doing. Doing is a form of knowing.

"The great end of life is not knowledge but action." T.H. Huxley[113]

The pragmatics of implementation is important in our society today. The days of academic theorizing no longer exist outside of implementation. The work of the philosopher gave way to the scientist. The work of the scientist is giving way to the DOER.

Our challenge lies in focusing our insights. Distraction from what is important is a continual obstacle.

The quantity of knowledge overwhelms wisdom. Choices, choices, choices. Knowing what in the knowledge stream is important and what will be important tomorrow is a monumental challenge. It can be a paralytic experience to step into the knowledge stream.

PATTERN RECOGNITION is the new critical skill. We need tools to socialize around knowledge. We need tools to store contextualized knowledge. We need tools to retrieve knowledge when needed (and in other cases, to bring it to our attention when we do not know that it is needed). We require the skills of a master—where one look can reveal insights, patterns, and opportunities not available to those new to the field.

The pattern reveals the value of knowledge. The pattern helps to guide elements required for future use. Pattern recognition is a skill reserved for those with a strong base in a field or discipline.

We are still learning how to be human in this environment. We do not yet fully understand how to manage, navigate, and create connections. We have spent our history dialoguing and communicating in primarily physical means.

What do we need to do in order to communicate in virtual spaces? How do we become human in this sphere?

Lack of structure is a consistent concern for participants in this space. We want to control, often forgetting that the new space is for conversation and connections.

We spend most of our time in debate/dialogue defining the space of the conversation, not the content. Creating the space determines the admissible content.

> Knowing is not enough; we must apply.
> Willing is not enough; we must do.
> Johann Wolfgang von Goethe [114]

Value is in the ability to create new connections based on existing and changing environments.

We can no longer create certainty. Instead, we create **patterns,** reflective of a particular point in time, then we act, but we must remain connected to the original source in order to stay current (and we should actually feed back into the original source so that both learn).

Figure 48. Pattern Recognition

To understand is to perceive patterns. Isaiah Berlin[115]

FEEDBACK is the key element in all healthy systems. The absence of feedback results in a lack of potential to adjust, acclimate, and adapt.

The addition of feedback allows the instructor to measure student progress, the organization to understand customer concerns, and management to understand employee needs. When applied to knowledge, it results in the progressive, spiral-like development of creation and co-creation.

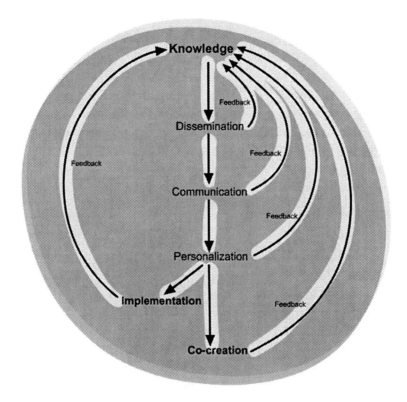

Figure 49. Knowledge Feedback

"*Organizations thrive on routine and the status quo. Professionals in organizations rely on the established systems in order to carry out their jobs with minimal resistance and stress. As a result, most people in companies today have not challenged themselves to learn something really different for a long time.*"
Daniel Goleman[116]

Change forces Change. The external pressure on environment and characteristics of knowledge requires new processes and models. To this end, ecologies and networks have been presented as new spaces and structures. But change is only valuable when it can be absorbed by an organism. Attempting too rapid a change process, while not preparing the organization to adapt and cope in the new environment, is a setup for disaster.

As presented through context-games and connectivism, the entire space of knowledge must be considered based on the pressures that inform and impact the whole structure. Isolationist or monochromatic views fail to unearth hidden concerns or potentially negative factors for organizations. Moving forward without accurately assessing the landscape may result in future failure. Moving forward while assuming the landscape has not changed (failing to build in reflexivity) presents similar prospects.

> *Traditional industrial corporations concentrate power in top management; yet many of the most successful corporations in recent years have implemented radical changes in governance systems...self-contained global enterprises, owning every part of the value chain from raw materials to retail, are giving way to networked organizations; enterprises that operate at high speeds.*
>
>

Senge et al.[117]

Attacking the problem (or opportunity) of organizational change with pre-planned solutions is insufficient. This is deeper than hiring a consultant. Our change plan needs to account for changes that occur as we begin to initiate change. The organization may be a very different structure mid-way through a change initiative. Adapt and react as changes occur. To pre-plan too far is to fail.

An integrated, holistic understanding of the organization's functioning is required. How does knowledge flow? What types of knowledge do we encounter? How do we meet our goals? How can we decentralize our communication? How can we open the doors of perception to enable an understanding of our deep beliefs (where we assume we are debating a concept on the surface, but are really battling deeper ideologies—forcing the issues into established structures of understanding and belief)?

How do we attend to the growing development from fixed answers to a robust, context-sensitive focus of each situation? Some questions have right answers. Others have answers that reshape the question as it is being answered. The concept being considered morphs as we come to know it and the environment (context) in which it exists, also changes.

> *The arts of doing and knowing, the valuation and the understanding of meaning, are thus seen to be only different aspects of extending our person into the subsidiary awareness of particulars which compose a whole.*

Michael Polanyi[118]

Practical implementation of the concepts addressed in this book requires a multi-faceted approach. The most effective approach is one which is adaptive and malleable, and holistic in scope.

The next several pages explores a five-domain implementation model (each with multiple stages) and numerous impacting factors.

This model is intended for system-wide application to corporate and educational spaces and structures. Connectivism implementation begins with creation of new organizational structures. New organizational structures then direct or allow for new affordances (see Figure 28). The combination of new spaces and structures and affordances permit the implementation of connectivist approaches to learning and knowledge flow in learning, communicating, collaborating, marketing, and other organizational activities.

The concepts expressed in this book can certainly be implemented outside of the involved process on the following pages. As presented throughout the text—the capacity for small scale, end-user driven activities are driving much of our societal change. Implementation can occur on a small scale, within individual classrooms, departments, or business units. A substantial challenge exists, as I have argued, with the structures of our organizations—which are simply not conducive to the changed characteristics and context of knowledge today. Optimal knowledge sharing within an organization, and greater capacity for individuals to learn, requires a large-scale redesign of the system itself.

Tinkering around the edges, in constant conflict with the balance of the organization, is a taxing and frustrating process. For these reasons, I have chosen to present a wide-scale implementation of connectivism, instead of smaller-scale views.

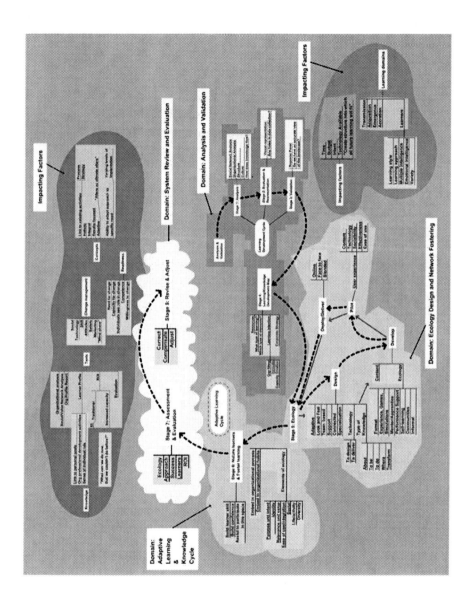

Figure 50 presents the elements of the **connectivism implementation cycle**, with subsequent images providing a detailed exploration of components.

The CONNECTIVISM DEVELOPMENT CYCLE (CDC) includes the following DOMAINS (AEASI):

1 . . . . Analysis and validation
2 . . . . Ecology and network design and fostering
3 . . . . Adaptive learning and knowledge cycle
4 . . . . System review and evaluation
5 . . . . Impacting factors

Domain 1:
ANALYSIS AND VALIDATION

Analysis and validation involves an organizational (or departmental) review of existing knowledge processes, habits, and employee competence. The initial analysis may include a broad-scale organizational analysis, as well as a locally-focused social network analysis. The analysis is then presented to a broad base of stakeholders (managers, employees, customers) to determine how accurately the analysis reflects the views of those who experience the organization in different ways.

Organizational knowledge is profiled according to domain, type, and state (see Figures 4, 5, and 8). Existing knowledge habits are contrasted with the manner in which knowledge should move through the organization (based on its characteristics).

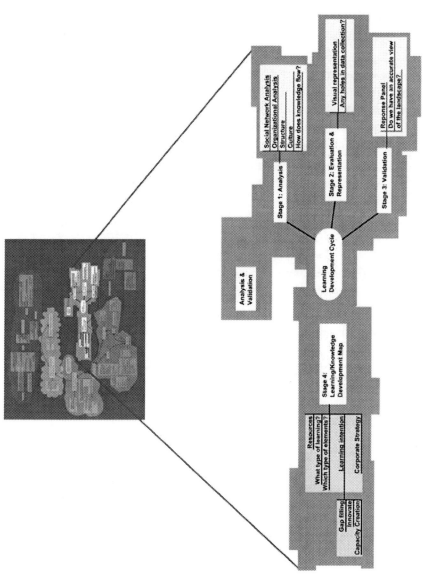

Figure 51.
Analysis and Validation

Domain 2:
NETWORK AND ECOLOGY DESIGN

The next stage of implementation involves the design and fostering of ecologies and networks. The creation of an ecology (see Figure 18) permits a broad-scale implementation of differing knowledge and learning experiences, permitting employees to achieve knowledge-based needs in a multi-faceted manner (through learning model), multiple ways (just-in-time, course-based—see Figure 17), and through multiple devices (computer, mobile device, classroom).

The four-stage process of design, develop, pilot, and deploy ensures that multiple factors and concerns are attended in advance of the learning "going live."

Learning networks, however, cannot be created in the same manner as an ecology. A network is a structure that individuals create on-their-own. Networks are external (nodes of information), and they are internal (how we represent knowledge). An organization can create a detailed external network (ensuring access to needed information), but the internal networks must be fostered and guided.

This domain can be implemented by trainers or educators within classes or courses. While much of the connectivism development model (CDM) is geared for creating systemic change (within a department or an entire organization), individuals can implement the second domain within teaching, learning, or knowledge-sharing environments.

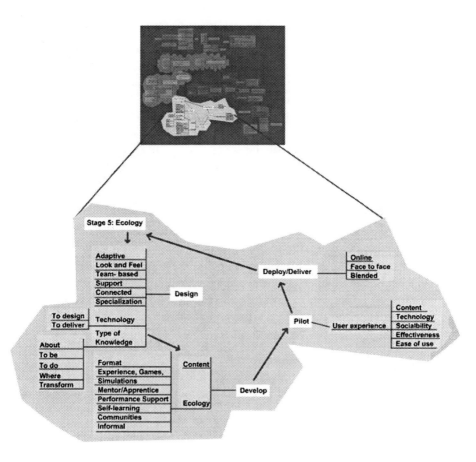

Figure 52. Ecology and Network Design

Domain 3:
ADAPTIVE KNOWLEDGE AND LEARNING CYCLE

After knowledge resources, ecologies, and networks have been developed (roughly shaped and hopefully co-created), each individual in the organization should create a personal knowledge plan to highlight the nature of the knowledge with which they work. This knowledge plan is not a rigid document, but more of a therapeutic evaluation of the factors impacting knowledge for the individual. The organization needs to provide an environment that will nurture the ecology and network formation activities for each employee (connected, obviously, to their personal knowledge plan).

In the domain of adaptive learning, organizations assist in building the skill-sets of employees so they are able to function in this new environment (digital, network, and ecological literacy are important skills to develop and foster).

Many spaces for knowledge sharing—whether digital or physical—suffer from lack of adoption. To foster adoption—and utilization—of ecologies and networks, organizations need to embed desired activities within organizational activities. Seven critical elements are required in healthy knowledge and learning ecologies:

> PURPOSE . . . Why does the space exist?
> What problem is it intended to solve?
> Or what ideal state is it intended to create?

> IDENTITY . . . Can each member create and control their own identity? Do individuals stay individual or do they blend with the group (silencing unique contributions)?

> RELEVANCE . . . Do members of the knowledge space see the value of involvement in their daily work or life? Does the purpose of the ecology align with their current interests, challenges, and opportunities?

> EASE OF USE & . . . Is the space easy to use for people who simply
> INTEGRATION want to connect with others, learn, and share knowledge? Are activities within the ecology integrated with regular work habits (access on a mobile device, or help icon on the desktop, or socialization built into existing instant messaging habits)?

SOCIAL . . .Does the ecology allow individuals to form relationships with others? Are identities discoverable (are participants able to find others of similar interests or workchallenges)?

LIFE & ACTIVITY . . .Does the ecology possess life? Is new knowledge explored, shared, expressed? Are new resources or functionality added? Do things change?

DIVERSITY . . .Does the ecology provide access to diverse viewpoints, opinions, and perspectives? Are individuals able to express their opinions honestly? Are fringe ideas considered and valued?

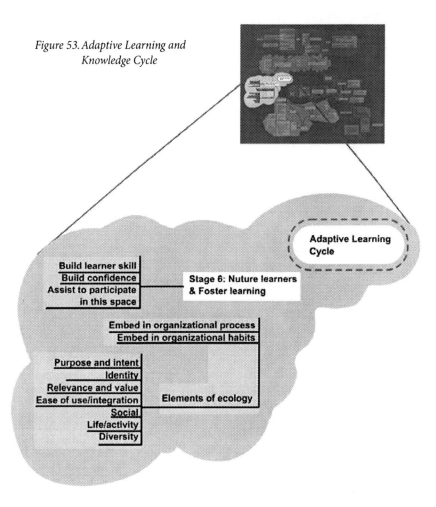

Figure 53. Adaptive Learning and Knowledge Cycle

Domain 4:
SYSTEMS & PATTERNS
REVIEW AND EVALUATION

Ongoing assessment and evaluation is required, as the organization adapts and adjusts knowledge approaches to reflect ongoing and core changes. **Evaluation** falls into broad categories:

1. The effectiveness of the ecology in achieving intended outcomes (innovation, increased customer service, increased knowledge sharing, quality of learning), and

2. Return on investment (reduced expenses, increased revenue, increased personal effectiveness of members involved in the ecology, organizational capacity to meet new challenges, organizational ability for adaptation and transformation).

The feedback generated through assessment and evaluation is used to revise and adjust the knowledge and learning ecology within the organization.

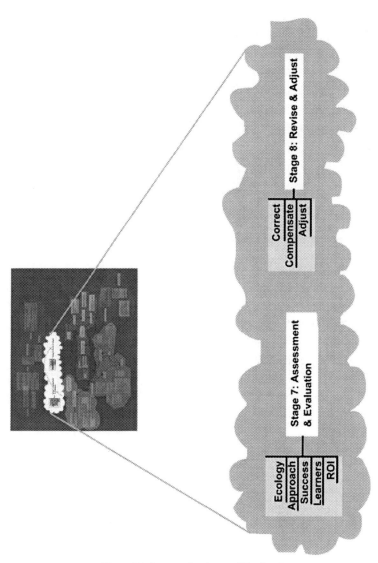

Figure 54. Systems Review and Evaluation

Domain 5:
IMPACTING FACTORS

The knowledge and learning development cycle is influenced by many factors which require consideration prior to, and during design.

These factors include:

- ▶ **TIME** available for development
- ▶ **BUDGET** for development and deployment
- ▶ **INTENT** of learning (solve an organizational challenge, build learner capacity for self-learning, innovation)
- ▶ **TECHNOLOGY** availability of end-users, and
- ▶ **COMPETENCE** of staff members to use new technology

The **domains of learning** (transmission, acquisition, emergence, accretion, see Figure 17) and the **attributes of learners** are important considerations at this stage. If the learning is intended to increase employee ability to innovate, but is delivered through structured models (course-based), the needed knowledge may not be readily encountered or acquired. A better model would be to focus on a combination of accretion and emergence learning—enabling employees to experience needed knowledge at a meta-cognitive level and through the course of their daily work activities. In order to be of greatest value, the required knowledge must be matched with the appropriate learning process or method.

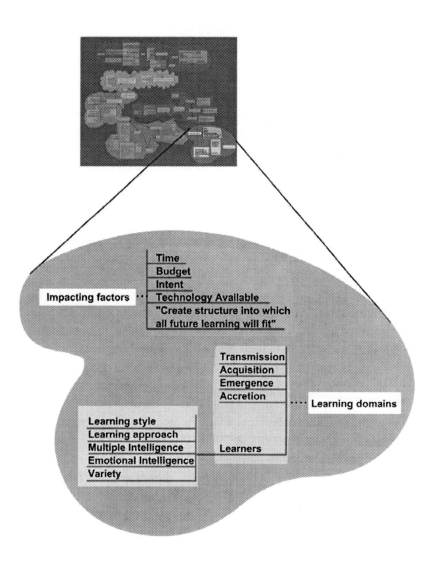

Figure 55. Impacting Factors (Learning and Knowledge Design)

The final set of impacting factors relates to broader organizational functioning. These include:

 * Tools Utilized　　 * Readiness　　 * Change Management
 * Guiding Principles & Concepts.

Tools Utilized refers to analysis, evaluation, and ROI metrics. These include matrices and analysis tools (to determine organizational climate, perceived need for change, confidence in leadership, trust among individuals, and other factors that create the climate and may influence the success of a knowledge ecology). Increasingly, social network analysis[119] is utilized to provide organizations with an overview with how knowledge flows through the enterprise.

Tools essentially facilitate the gathering of appropriate information representing the current reality. The items assessed must be relevant (contextually appropriate) to the existing ecology, intended outcome of a healthy ecology (learning focus), and esired future state.

Readiness addresses the potential for change within a department, school, university, or corporation. If employees do not feel change is required, or if they recognize the need for change but lack confidence in meeting those needs, most attempts for change will fail. In an ideal climate, individuals must see the value of change, see their own role in the process, be willing to adopt new approaches, and possess the competence to move forward with change.

Change Management addresses the process and challenge of moving to new methods (namely interacting within an ecology and creating networks for knowledge dispersion). Once an accurate image of current barriers (and opportunities) for change management have been explored, a *marketing* process is adopted to ensure "mind share" and general understanding of the role and value of knowledge sharing and participation in the ecology.

The adoption of an ecological approach to learning and knowledge (sharing, dissemination, or creation) is guided by several key concepts:

1. **Holistic:** Diversely representing the situation, allowing multiple perspectives and views

2. **Adaptive:** Able to adjust and change as the environment changes.

3. **Linked** to existing habits, activities, process, and tools.

4. **Results focused:** Ensuring that the ecology (which will be messy and chaotic) achieves intended targets or desired outcomes. As mentioned earlier, our challenge today is to achieve clear aims through decentralized means.

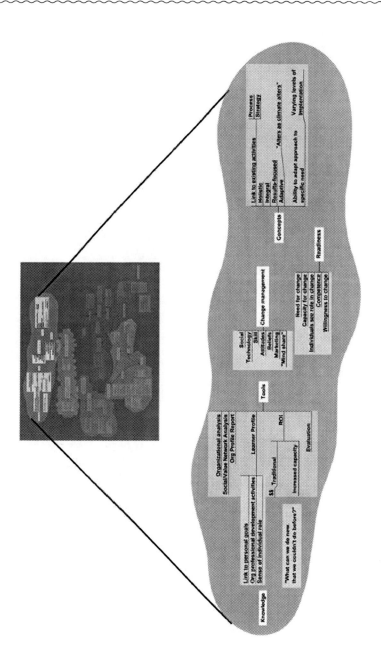

Figure 56. Impacting Factors: Implementation

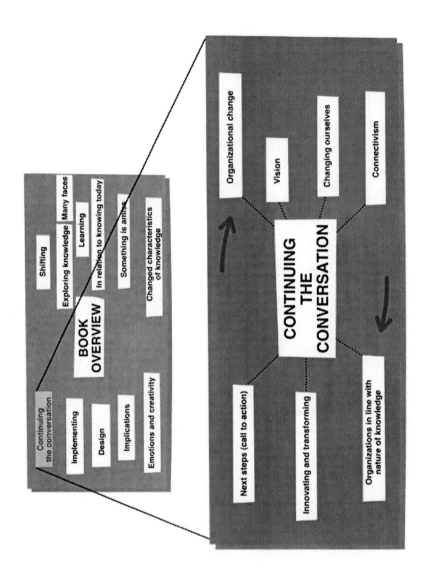

Figure 57.
Continuing the Conversation

Continuing . . .
THE CONVERSATION

The challenge for organizational change does not rest in technology, or creating complex implementations. We need a vision for organizational design that aligns with the changed context and characteristics of knowledge. Our organizational spaces and structures have been designed to serve an era that no longer exists. Knowledge, unlike physical products, is not subject to paucity. Innovation and continued development requires effective flow of knowledge throughout an organization. Instead of preserving (or hoarding), sharing, and connecting create value.

We have to unlearn what no longer serves us well—to jettison the mindsets formed by existing in only physical worlds. We also have to learn new models, new concepts, and new visions for what is possible. We are still using our tools to serve our old tasks. We should be about entirely new tasks.

…but the way forward is not to delve into our toolkit of existing solutions and applying them to problems taking a known shape. We must walk forward with an adaptive mindset—recognizing pattern changes and adjusting as the environment itself adjusts.

We walk a balance between bending knowledge to serve our organizational needs and permitting knowledge to emerge (then acting on the patterns created by the emergence of knowledge). As I have tried to communicate throughout this book, no single solution and approach will always be right. Our actions should be based on a complete understanding of the situation before us, not only on an understanding of our kit of templated solutions. The focus must shift from what we know to what the patterns are as created by the continual process of developing knowledge.

The changes discussed in this book do not apply exclusively to online or technology-enabled environments. A reordering of our physical spaces within organizations and schools is required. Whether online, or in physical spaces and structures, the capacity for effective knowledge flow, optimal opportunities for connection, recombination, and re-creation is vital.

We want to belong. We want to achieve. We want to pull back the curtain of the unknown. But we are people. We are insecure. We doubt ourselves. Social groups have power because they cover our individual weaknesses.

Knowledge is functioning according to new characteristics in a changed environment and context. It forms rapidly, disperses quickly. It is chaotic, messy. It is shaped by many hands. What shall our vision be? Short-term, our organizational vision needs to reflect a desire to align our spaces and structures with the nature of knowledge and learning.

To function in the new world of knowledge, we need to see the power of connections—connectivism and connective knowledge. Sense-making, pattern recognition, suspended certainty—these are our needed skills. As our physical, industrial era was defined by the movement of goods (from raw material to end consumer), so too knowledge will be defined by its movement through our corporations and society. The conduits, the gatekeepers, the filters of industrial implementations of knowledge are losing grip. As knowledge floods the landscape, we become our own gatekeepers. The opportunity requires new skills and tasks.

Our first work is to equip and prepare ourselves to handle the new nature and flow of knowledge.

WHAT IS DIFFERENT TOMORROW MORNING?

To know of knowledge changes, to understand technological and societal trends, provides little value unless it leads to action. I recommend the following as steps toward using the content of this book:

1. Join Knowing Knowledge newsletter (or subscribe to the blog feed) and contribute to the re-writing of this book in the wiki. www.knowingknowledge.com

2. Become active in the conversation of organizational (spaces and structures) change (within your company, industry, and society)

3. Build a personal network for support as you move toward change within your organization (form a global support net work). Focus on fostering an ecology and developing skills in network formation.

4. Focus on the ecologies (spaces) and networks (structures) that form the foundation of markets, media, corporations, schools, and society itself. The future belongs to the network aware. Chaos and order … tension and harmony … centralization and decentralization—these comprise the whole, with no one entity superceding the other in all situations.

A holistic, integral approach to thinking, learning, and knowledge is required as our society grows in complexity.

The opportunity for change is tremendous. Opportunities to restructure organizations and society are rare. Yet periodically—in periods of substantial social, technological, or ideological change—we have the opportunity to remake our existence, to rewrite the inefficiencies of antiquated modes of operation. With vision, foresight, and awareness of change, we can move forward with a model that will serve humanity well. We exist in such a time. If we are able to loose our faulty view of control-in-advance and embrace an adaptive, flow-view of knowledge, we have the capability to restructure our organizations to best serve our learners, employees, and customers.

NOTES

1 Knowledge Quotes. (2006). *Knowledge Quotations: Richard Cecil.* Retrieved Septe mber 1, 2006, from http://www.wisdomquotes.com/cat_ knowledge. html

2 Drucker, P. F. (2003). The Essential Drucker: The Best of Sixty Years of Peter Drucker's Essential Writings on Management. New York: Harper Business.

3 Comments from reviewers have been integrated with the text, but without direct attribution for ideas (beyond mention of reviewers in the preface). I should note Stephen Downes' comments on the initial section of the text in clarifying knowledge (as subject to description, not definition), as well as the discussion on information/knowledge distinctions.

4 A blog is a simple web page, with thoughts and commentary from one or more individuals. Entries are dated (in reverse chronological order) and categorized. Blogs are usually combined with RSS (an XML format) to allow individuals to read blog posts in their aggregator, rather than visiting each website. Stephen Downes provides a thorough overview of educational blogging: http://www.educause.edu/pub/er/erm04/erm0450. asp A basic overview of blogging itself is available from George Siemens: http://www.elearnspace.org/Articles/blogging_part_1.htm.

Both links retrieved September 1, 2006.

Will Richardson has produced an excellent text for educators. Richardson, W. (2006). *Blogs, wikis, podcasts and other powerful web tools for classrooms.* Thousand Oaks, CA: Corwin Press.

5 A wiki, loosely defined, is a web page that anyone can edit. One of the most popular wikis is the user-created Wikipedia (www.wikipedia.org) Brian Lamb provides an excellent overview of wikis:

Lamb, B. (2004, September/October). Wide open spaces: Wikis, ready or not. *EDUCAUSE Review, 39*(5), 36–48. Retrieved September 1, 2006, from http://www.educause.edu/pub/er/erm04/erm0452.asp

6 Tags are essentially end-user created metadata. Instead of an author or publisher providing a description or classification of a resource, tags allow end users to describe resources in ways they themselves find meaningful. Social book marking is a related concept where the combined "book marking" activities of many are presented, revealing patterns of importance (based on how popular a resource is in the public mind).

Mathes, A. (2004). *Folksonomies - Cooperative classification and communication through shared metadata.* Retrieved September 1, 2006, from http://www.adammathes.com/academic/computer-mediated-communication/folksonomies.html

Clay Shirky provides a thorough overview of tags and social book marking in relation to traditional classification schemes:

Shirky, C. (2005). *Ontology is overrated: Categories, links, and tags.* Retrieved September 1, 2006, from http://shirky.com/writings/ontology_overrated.html

7 A podcast is an audio file available for download to a desktop or audio player (MP3 or iPod). Audio clips can range from a few minutes to multi-hour lectures or interviews.

8 Video logs are based on similar philosophy as blogs—the ability for anyone to affordably publish media. A video log is generally a short video file (five-ten minutes) available for download or viewing online. For example, Ze Frank (www.zefrank.com/theshow) produces a regular podcast, having acquired significant viewer base in only a few months.

9 Harris, K. (1995). *Collected quotes of Albert Einstein.* Retrieved September 1, 2006, http://rescomp.stanford.edu/~cheshire/EinsteinQuotes.html.

10 I am well aware of the irony of ranting against structure and hierarchy, and then subjecting readers to static, linear graphics. Beyond producing *Knowing Knowledge* as a multi-media resource, this seemed like a necessary compromise.

11 Kuhn, T. S. (1962). *The structure of scientific revolutions.* Chicago: University of Chicago Press.

12 Biederman, I., & Vessel, E. A. (2006). Perceptual pleasure and the brain. American Scientist, 94(3), 247. Irving Biederman and Edward A. Vessel suggest "visual input activates receptors in the parts of the brain associated with pleasure and reward, and that the brain associates new images with old while also responding strongly to new ones. Using functional MRI imaging and other findings, they are exploring how human beings are 'infovores' whose brains love to learn." Our brain appears to "crave information" (1).

13 Benkler, Y. (2006). *The wealth of networks* (p. 1). New Haven, CT: Yale University Press.

14 Adorno, T. W. (1984). Minima moralia: *Reflections from damaged life.* London: Verso.

15 Bandura, A. (1985). *Social foundations of thought and action: A social cognitive theory* (p. 23). Upper Saddle River, NJ: Prentice Hall. Offers "triadic reciprocality" of interaction. He includes the domains: behavior, cognitive, and personal factors, as well as environment influences.

The three elements work together, influencing and shaping each other.

In a similar sense, the four domains provided in this text (cognitive, social, emotional, and spiritual) exist in an interplay of interaction and functioning.

16 Watts, D. (2003). Six degrees (p. 273). New York: W. W. Norton.

17 *Great thoughts about physics*. (n.d.). Max Planck. Retrieved September 1, 2006, from http://www.helical-structures.org/great_thoughts. htm

18 Durkheim, E. (1995). *Elementary forms of the religious life* (trans. Karen Fields). New York: Free Press.

19 Boghossian, P. (2006). *Fear of knowledge* (p. 2). New York: Oxford University Press.

20 Ackoff, R. L. (1989). From data to wisdom. *Journal of Applied Systems Analysis, 16*, 3-9.

21 Nonaka, I., & Takeuchi, H. (1995). *The knowledge creation company.* New York: Oxford University Press.

22 Popper, K. (1978). *Three worlds.* Retrieved September 1, 2006, from http://www.tannerlectures.utah.edu/lectures/popper80.pdf

23 Weick, K. E., Sutcliff, K. M., & Obstfeld, D. (2005). Organizing and the process of sense-making. *Organization Science, 16*(2), 409-421

24 QuoteWorld. (2006). *Joseph Joubert Quotes.* Retrieved September 1, 2006, from http://www.quoteworld.org/quotes/7433

25 Boghossian, P. (2006). *Fear of knowledge.* New York: Oxford University Press.

26 Siemens, G. (2005). *Connectivism: A learning theory for a digital age.* Retrieved September 1, 2006, from http://www.itdl.org/Journal/Jan_05/article01.htm

27 Downes, S. (2005). *Connective knowledge.* Retrieved September 1, 2006, from http://www.downes.ca/cgi-bin/page.cgi?post=33034

28 Bloor, D. (1983). *Wittgenstein: A social theory of knowledge* (pp. 23-49). New York: Columbia University Press.

29 Siemens, G. (2006, June). *Networks: Revisiting objective/subjective.* Retrieved September 1, 2006, from http://www.connectivism. ca/blog/67

30 Johnson, S. (2001). *Emergence* (p. 42). New York: Scribner.

31 Snowden, D. (2006). Special people. *Cognitive Edge* (50). Retrieved September 1, 2006, from http://www.cognitive-edge.com/2006/09/ special_people.php

32 Gopnik, A. (2002). What children will teach scientists. In J. Brockman (Ed.), *The next fifty years – Science in the first half of the twenty-first century*. New York: Vintage.

33 Downes, S. (2004). (2004). *New directions in learning*. Retrieved September 1, 2006, from http://www.downes.ca/files/NDL.ppt

34 Toffler, A., & Toffler, H. (2006). *Revolutionary wealth* (p. 313). New York: Alfred A. Knopf.

35 Oblinger, D., & Oblinger, J. (Eds.). (2005). Is it age or IT: First steps toward understanding the net generation. In *Educating the Net Generation* Retrieved September 1, 2006, from http://www.educause.edu/ir/library/pdf/pub7101b.pdf

36 Meyer, C., & Davis, S. (2003). *It's alive*. New York: Crown Business.

37 Gleick, J. (1987). *Chaos: The making of a new science*. New York: Penguin Books

38 Santa Fe Institute (2006) is a leading research lab, focusing on complex adaptive systems. Their mandate: "The Santa Fe Institute is devoted to creating a new kind of scientific research community, one emphasizing multidisciplinary collaboration in pursuit of understanding the common themes that arise in natural, artificial, and social systems. This unique scientific enterprise attempts to uncover the mechanisms that underlie the deep simplicity present in our complex world." (1). Retrieved September 1, 2006, from http://www.santafe.edu/

39 Rocha, L. (1998). Selected self-organization. In S. Salthe, G. Van de Vijver, & M. Delpos (Eds.), *Evolutionary systems: Biological and epistemological perspectives on selection and self-organization* (pp. 341-358). Retrieved September 1, 2006, from http://informatics.indiana.edu/rocha/ps/ises.pdf

Luis Mateus Rocha presents self-organization as "the spontaneous formation of well organized structures, patterns, or behaviors, from random initial conditions" (p. 3).

40 The concept of knowledge resting in non-human appliances (mediated by artificial intelligence or directed by intelligent agents) is controversial. As with the discussion on context-games, how one defines knowledge largely determines whether one will accept this definition. As mentioned in the preface, I have largely avoided the use of the word *information* in this text. It could be well argued that all knowledge is simply varying shades of information, and information itself is transformed into knowledge when we have a personal relationship with it (i.e., we internalize information).

This discussion, from my perspective, is unnecessary for the purpose of this book. In order to have any practical discussion of information and knowledge, we need to discuss it as if it is something that a) describes some aspect of the world, and b) something on which we can act. This simple definition provides the basis for viewing knowledge as being able to reside in non-human appliances.

41 Gates, B. (2005). *What's wrong with U.S. high schools—and how we can make them better.* Retrieved September 1, 2006, from http://www.eschoolnews.com/news/showstory.cfm?ArticleID=5586

42 Samuel Johnson sound bite page. (2006). Retrieved September 1, 2006, from http://www.samueljohnson.com/twokinds.html

43 This figure depicts learning as consisting of accretion, transmission, acquisition, and emergence domains, (these terms do not appear to have a clear origin, though they have been used by Wilson (1997) and Calhoun (n.d.) without clear attribution to the originating source):

Calhoun, G., Jr. (n.d.). Praxis notes. Retrieved September 1, 2006, from http://www.cheyney.edu/pages/?p=163

Wilson, L. O. (1997). *New view of learning: Types of learning.* Retrieved September 1, 2006, from http://www.uwsp.edu/education/lwilson/learning/typesofl.htm

44 Kirschner, P. A., Sweller, J., & Clark, R. E. (In press). Why minimally guided instruction does not work. *Educational Psychologist* (January 2006). The authors state that minimally-guided instruction (a variant of self-directed learning) is less effective than guided instruction because of the structure of "human cognitive architecture." Many factors impact (context game) the environment, in which guided/minimally-guided models are implemented. It is worth noting that minimally-guided instruction is still better than no instruction at all. Like many businesses have discovered, face-to-face meetings are superior to online meetings (the richness of the human space, contact, and interaction). In many situations; however, it is not financially feasible or even practical to bring all parties together face-to-face. An online session or video conference works well in these cases.

45 Romesin, H. M., & Bunnell, P. (1998). Biosphere, Homosphere, and robosphere: What has that to do with Business? *Society for Organizational Learning.* Retrieved September 1, 2006, from http://www.solonline.org/res/wp/maturana/index.html

46 Facts, truth, knowledge, and beliefs are interrelated, but each possesses different attributes. Facts are elements of the world which are

independent of us (Boghossian, 2006, p. 20); for example, dinosaurs once existed on earth. A belief is a mental state that may or may not be true (Boghossian, p. 10); for example, the cause of inflation in an economy, or the motivations of an opposing political party.

Truth (see http://en.wikipedia.org/wiki/Truth Retrieved September 1, 2006) is commonly viewed as a judgment or valuation contrasting facts and belief (justification). If a belief is justified and supported by fact, it can be described as being truthful.

47 Goleman, D., Boyatzis, R., & McKee, A. (2002). *Primal leadership.* Boston: Harvard Business School.

48 Snowden, D. (2006, August 13). *Tales of a wikipedia virgin.* Cognitive Edge. Retrieved September 1, 2006, from http://www.cognitive-edge.com/2006/08/tales_of_a_wikipedia_virgin.php

49 Weinberger, D. (2005, June 27). *The new shape of knowledge.* Retrieved September 1, 2006, from http://www.hyperorg.com/blogger/mtarchive/004153.html

50 Vaill, P. B. (1996). *Learning as a way of being* (p. 30). San Francisco, CA: Jossey- Bass.

51 Downes, S. (2005, December 22). *An introduction to connective knowledge.* Retrieved September 1, 2006, from http://www.downes.ca/cgi-bin/page.cgi?post=33034

52 Rock, D., & Schwartz, J. (2006, August 7). The neuroscience of leadership. *strategy+business*(43), 4. Retrieved September 1, 2006 PROVIDE URL

53 Stephenson, K. (n.d.). *What knowledge tears apart, networks make whole.* Retrieved September 1, 2006, from http://www.netform.com/html/icf.pdf

54 Strogatz, S. (2003). Sync (p. 59). New York: Hyperion.

55 Wisdom Quotes. (2006). *Mark Van Doren.* Retrieved September 1, 2006, from http://www.wisdomquotes.com/002867.html

56 Surowiecki, J. (2004). *The wisdom of crowds.* New York: Doubleday.

57 Anderson, C. (2006, April 10). Mainstream Media Meltdown. Retrieved September 1, 2006, from http://longtail.typepad.com/the_long_tail/2005/04/media_meltdown.html Chris Anderson provides an overview of media decline in 2005: music sales down 21%, TV audience has declined by 30% since 1985, and newspapers show a continual decline.

57 Driscoll, M. (2000). *Psychology of learning for instruction.* Needham Heights, MA: Allyn & Bacon.

58 A variation of Marshall McLuhan's statement: "We look at the present through a rear-view mirror. We march backwards into the future." From: McLuhan, M., Fiore, Q., & Agel, J. (1967). *The medium is the massage: An inventory of effects.* Corte Madera, CA: Gingko Press.

59 Moore, J. F. (2003). *The second superpower rears its beautiful head.* Retrieved September 1, 2006, from http://cyber.law.harvard.edu/people/jmoore/secondsuperpower.html

60 Stacey, R., & Griffin, D. (Eds.). (2005). *A complexity perspective on researching organizations: Taking experience seriously.* New York: Taylor & Francis Group.

61 Chesterton, G. K. (1994). *Orthodoxy.* Wheaton, IL: Harold Shaw.

62 Sutton, B. (2006, July 17). *Strong opinions, weakly held.* Retrieved September 1, 2006, from http://bobsutton.typepad.com/my_weblog/2006/07/strong_opinions.html

63 Restak, R. (2003). *The new brain* (p. 40). New York: Rodale.

64 *A complexity science primer.* (n.d.). Review of the book *Edgeware: Lessons from complexity science for health care leaders* by Brenda Zimmerman, Curt Lindberg, Paul Plsek. Retrieved month day, year, from http://www.pms.ac.uk/healthcomplexity/files/Primer%20on%20Complexity.doc Retrieved September 1, 2006

65 Joining Dots. (n.d.). *One liners: Jack Welch* (6). Retrieved September 1, 2006, from http://www.joiningdots.net/library/Research/one_liners.html

66 Wikimania. (2006). David Weinberger in keynote to Wikimania: August 11, 2006. Retrieved September 1, 2006, from http://wikimania2006.wikimedia.org/wiki/Image:Wikimania_20060806_David_Weinberger-_What%27s_happening_to_knowledge.ogg

67 Locke, C., Levine, R., Searls, D. & Weinberger, D. (2001). *The cluetrain manifesto.* New York: Perseus Publishing.

68 Barabási, A. (2002). *Linked: The new science of networks* (p. 170). Cambridge, MA: Perseus Publishing, discusses how only a small percentage of webpages link to opposing viewpoints. We are creating spaces of social and political isolation, where our ideas are unquestioned.

69 Linden Research. (2006). *Second life. Your world. Your imagination.* Retrieved September 6, 2006, from http://secondlife.com/ Second Life is among the first generation of game-based virtual worlds, allowing individuals to create their own identity and build an online existence.

My Virtual Life. (2006, May 1). *Business Week online.* Retrieved September 6, 2006, from http://www.businessweek.com/magazine/content06_18/b3982001.htm My Virtual Life details the merging physical and virtual worlds. Individuals can purchase or sell property, hold concerts, book signings, and other activities previously confined to physical spaces.

70 Bowie, D. (1971). Changes. On *Hunky Dory* [record]. New York: RCA.

71 MSNBC News. (n.d.) *Rewiring the brain.* Retrieved September 1, 2006, from http://web.mit.edu/~davidf/www/MSNBC_Rewiring_the_brain.htm

72 Restak, R. (1995). *Brainscapes: An introduction to what neuroscience has learned about the structure, function, and abilities of the brain* (pp. 134-135). New York: Hyperion Books.

72 Swearingen, K., Charles, P., Good, N., Jordan, L. L., Lyman, P., Pal., J., & Varian, H. R. (2003). *How much information?* Retrieved September 1, 2006, from http://www2.sims.berkeley.edu/research/projects/how-much-info-2003

74 Hagel, J. (2004, November 1). *Return on attention and infomediaries.* Retrieved September 6, 2006, from http://edgeperspectives.typepad.com/edge_perspectives/2005/11/return_on_atten.html John Hagel discusses attention as the real source of tension in an information-rich world. We have finite limitations placed on our ability to pay attention.

75 Sahasrabuddhe, H.V. (n.d.). *Half-life of knowledge.* Retrieved September 8, 2006, from http://www.it.iitb.ac.in/~hvs/HalfLife/HalfLifeSlides.ppt. The concept of half-life of knowledge is controversial. The term half-life refers to "The time required for the quantity of a chemical, drug or radioisotope to fall to half."

Knowledge has different properties than physical objects. Similarities of decay (or depreciation), however, can be noted in knowledge-spaces where new discoveries are being made regularly. The existing knowledge is gradually subject to decay (obsolescence) as new research and innovation replaces existing knowledge.

76 Knight, P. T. (1997). *The half-life of knowledge and structural reform of the education sector for the global knowledge-based economy.* Retrieved September 6, 2006, from http://www.knight-moore.com/pubs/halflife.html

77 Massachusetts Institute of Technology. (n.d.) *OpenCourseWare.* Retrieved September 1, 2006, from http://ocw.mit.edu/index.html Initiative provides free, open access to educational material for "educators, students, and self-learners around the world" (1).

78 McLuhan, M. (1967). *The medium is the massage: An inventory of effects.* Corte Madera, CA: Gingko Press.

79 Noguchi, Y. (2005, July 8). Camera phones lend immediacy to images of disaster *Washington Post,* p. A16. Retrieved September 6, 2006, from http://www.washingtonpost.com/wp-dyn/content/article/2005/07/07/AR2005070701522.html

80 Bryan, L. L., & Joyce, C. (2005). *The 21st century organization.* Retrieved September 1, 2006, from http://www.mckinseyquarterly.com/ab_g.aspx?ar=1628

81 Joint Information Systems Committee. (2006). *Designing space for effective learning: A guide to 21st century learning space design* (p. 30). Retrieved September 1, 2006, from http://www.jisc.ac.uk/uploaded_documents/JISClearningspaces.pdf

82 Siemens, G. (2003). *Learning ecologies, communities, and networks.* Retrieved September 1, 2006, from http://www.elearnspace.org/Articles/learning_communities.htm

83 Spool, J. M. (2006). *An interview with Barry Schwartz.* Retrieved September 1, 2006, from http://www.uie.com/events/uiconf/2006/articles/schwartz_interview/

84 Morris, D. M., Mason, J., Robson, R., Lefrier, P., & Collier, G. (2003). *A revolution in knowledge sharing.* Retrieved September 1, 2006, from http://www.educause.edu/ir/library/pdf/erm0350.pdf

85 William Butler Yeats Poem: The Second Coming. First printed in The Dial, 1920.

86 Minsky, M. (1985). *The society of mind* (p. 17). New York: Simon & Schuster.

87 Johnson, S. (2001). *Emergence* (p. 21). New York: Scribner.

88 Landauer, T. K., & Dumais, S. T. (1997). *A solution to Plato's problem: The latent semantic analysis theory of acquisition, induction and representation of knowledge.* Retrieved September 1, 2006, from http://lsa.colorado.edu/papers/plato/plato.annote.html.

89 Minsky, M. (1985). *The society of mind* (p. 17). New York: Simon & Schuster

90 Kurtz, C. F., & Snowden, D. J. (2003). *The new dynamics of strategy.* Retrieved September 1, 2006, from http://www.research.ibm.com/journal/sj/423/kurtz.pdf

91 Thinkexist.com (1996). *Abraham Maslow quotes* (1). Retrieved September 1, 2006, from http://en.thinkexist.com/quotation/if_the_only_tool_you_have_is_a_hammer-you_tend_to/221060.html

92 Ratey, J. J. (2001). *A user's guide to the brain.* New York: Vintage Books.

93 Smith, A. (2006). *An inquiry into the nature and causes of the wealth of nations* [[EBook #3300]. Retrieved September 1, 2006, from http://www.gutenberg.org/etext/3300

94 Postman, N. (1995). *The end of education* (p. 7). New York: Vintage Books.

95 Ralph Waldo Emerson: Progress of culture. (1867). *Phi Beta Kappa Address, July 18, 1867*

96 BrainyQuote. (2006). *Blaise Pascal Quotes* (1). Retrieved September 6, 2006, from http://www.brainyquote.com/quotes/authors/b/blaise_pascal.html

97 Talbott, S. (2005). *Where we have come to (Part 1).* Retrieved September 1, 2006, from http://www.netfuture.org/2005/Oct2505_165.html

98 Pink, D. (2005). *A whole new mind: Moving from information age to conceptual age.* New York: Riverhead Books.

99 Wikipedia. (n.d.). *Creativity.* Retrieved September 1, 2006, from http://en.wikipedia.org/wiki/Creativity

100 Gurteen Knowledge Website. (2006). Peter F. Drucker quoted on conserving institutions and change. Retrieved September 1, 2006, from http://www.gurteen.com/gurteen/gurteen.nsf/id/X004EA36E/

101 McLuhan, M. (1994). *Understanding media: The extensions of man* (MIT Press Edition) Cambridge, MA: MIT.

102 RFID and privacy (2004, May 28). Retrieved September 6, 2006, from http://www.infoworld.com/article/04/05/28/HNrfidprivacy_1.html Radio frequency identification (RFID) chips demonstrate the battle of privacy and advancement of technology. The ability for RFID to control and monitor supplies can result in significant advantages to corporations and governments.
Muta, M. (2006, July 6). The promise and opportunity of RFID in hospitality. Retrieved September 6, 2006, from http://www.microsoft.com/industry/hospitality/businessvalue/rfidopportunityarticle.mspx Hotels are starting to use RFID tags to track supplies and manage cashless purchases with guests. But with increased freedom comes the threat of increase ability for surveillance or monitoring.

103 Information Literacy Competency Standards for Higher Education. (The Association of College and Research Libraries) has defined information literacy as ability to "recognize when information is needed and have the ability to locate, evaluate, and effectively use needed information." Their list of standards provide a base for specific skills surrounding information acquisition, evaluation, and use.

104 Beinhocker, E. D. (2006). *The origin of wealth. Evolution, complexity, and the radical remaking of economics* (p. 17). Boston: Harvard Business School Press.

105 Johnson, S. (2001). *Emergence.* New York: Scribner.

106 Cross, J. (n.d.). *Informal learning blog.* Retrieved September 1, 2006, from http://informl.com/

107 Hutchins, E. (2000). *Distributed cognition.* Retrieved September 1, 2006, from http://eclectic.ss.uci.edu/~drwhite/Anthro179a/DistributedCognition.pdf

108 Spivey, M., Richardson D., & Fitneva, S. (2004). Thinking outside the brain: Spatial indices to visual and linguistic information. In J. Henderson & F. Ferreira (Eds.), *The Interface of vision language and action.* New York: Psychology Press.

109 Wisdom Quotes. (2006). *Blaise Pascal quote.* Retrieved September 1, 2006, from http://www.wisdomquotes.com/cat_doubtuncertainty.html

110 Technologies are emerging which serve this function. RSS feeds in news sites and blogs provide a two-way flow that permits an individual to stay abreast of changes by subscribing to an information source. The potential of this technology is still in the initial formative stages, but early indications suggest that it could significantly change how we experience and relate to information and knowledge.

111 Aggregators (like www.bloglines.com) permit individuals to bring together various information sources into a centralize environment.

112 In Ferris, A. (translator). (1962). The voice of the master. In *A second treasury of Kahlil Gibran.* Englewood, NJ: Lyle Stuart.

113 Bartleby.com. (2006). *Thomas Henry Huxley quotations* (7). Retrieved September 1, 2006, from http://www.bartleby.com/100/530.7.html

114 BrainyQuotes. (2006). *Johann Wolfgang von Goethe* quotes. Retrieved September 1, 2006, from http://www.brainyquote.com/quotes/quotes/j/johannwolf161315.html

115 Quotations Books. (2006). *Sir Isaiah Berlin quotations.* Retrieved September 1, 2006, from http://www.quotationsbook.com/quotes/40154/view

116 Goleman, D. (2002). Primal leadership. *Realizing the power of emotional intelligence* (p. 226). Boston: Harvard Business School Press.

117 Senge, P., Kleiner, A., Roberts, C., Ross, R., Roth, G., & Smith, B. (1999). *The dance of change* (p. 361). New York: Doubleday.

118 Polanyi, M. (1958). *Personal knowledge: Towards a post-critical philosophy* (p. 65). Chicago: University of Chicago Press.

119 Social network analysis is the process of identifying (and in some cases, measuring) the social connections which exist within an organization or group (Valdis Krebs, Orgnet http://www.orgnet. com/sna.html, *How to do social network analysis*). Often, knowledge flows through a social network very different from the one created by management in the form of an organizational chart. Key nodes can play a role in knowledge distribution well beyond what their position in the organizational chart suggests. Rob Cross (*The hidden power of social networks*, 2004, Harvard Business School Publishing Corporation, p. ix) states that these nodes (people) "add context, interpretation, and meaning as they receive information and pass it along". The anticipated structure of a corporation (defined by organization or hierarchical charts) may not capture the true manner in which work is completed. Even when knowledge flows through established pathways/hierarchies, the injection of "context, interpretation, and meaning" alters the message and interpretation.

TABLES

FIGURES

INDEX